INDIAN JUSTICE

Also by Grant Foreman (published by the
University of Oklahoma Press)

(ed.) *A Traveler in Indian Territory: The Journal of
Ethan Allen Hitchcock* (1930)
*Indians & Pioneers: The Story of the American
Southwest Before 1830* (1930, 1936)
*Indian Removal: The Emigration of the Five
Civilized Tribes of Indians* (1932)
Advancing the Frontier, 1830–1860 (1933)
*The Five Civilized Tribes: Cherokee, Chickasaw,
Choctaw, Creek, Seminole* (1934)
Down the Texas Road (1936)
Fort Gibson: A Brief History (1936)
(ed.) *Adventure on Red River*, by Randolph B.
Marcy (1937)
Sequoyah (1938)
Marcy and the Gold Seekers (1939)
(ed.) *A Pathfinder in the Southwest*, by A. W.
Whipple (1941)
A History of Oklahoma (1942)
Muskogee: The Biography of an Oklahoma Town
(1943)

Also by Rennard Strickland (published by the
University of Oklahoma Press)

*Fire and the Spirits: Cherokee Law from Clan to
Court* (1975)
The Indians in Oklahoma (1980)
(ed.) *Oklahoma Memories*, with Anne Hodges
Morgan (1981)

INDIAN JUSTICE

A Cherokee Murder Trial
at Tahlequah
in 1840

As Reported by

JOHN HOWARD PAYNE

Edited by

Grant Foreman

Foreword by

Rennard Strickland

UNIVERSITY OF OKLAHOMA PRESS
NORMAN

Library of Congress-Cataloging-in-Publication Data

Payne, John Howard, 1791–1852.
   Indian justice : a Cherokee murder trial at Tahlequah in 1840 / as reported by John Howard Payne ;
edited by Grant Foreman ; foreword by Rennard
Strickland.
      p. cm.
   Includes bibliographical references and index.
   ISBN 0-8061-3420-8 (pbk. : alk. paper)
   1. Smith, Archilla, d. 1841—Trials, litigation, etc.
   2. Trials (Murder)—Oklahoma—Tahlequah.
   3. Cherokee law. 4. MacIntosh, John, d. 1839.
   I. Foreman, Grant, 1869–1953. II. Title.

KF228.S55 P39 2002
345.73′05523′0976688—dc21

                                          2001055698

      1   2   3   4   5   6   7   8   9   10

CONTENTS

ILLUSTRATIONS

Following page 48

FOREWORD

In Search of Justice: A Chapter in Native American Social and Legal History

On that crisp fall weekend when much of the nation was viewing the televised confrontation between Supreme Court nominee Clarence Thomas and University of Oklahoma law professor Anita Hill, the Cherokees gathered in Tahlequah, Oklahoma, to address another legal issue. The tribe had come together for the state and county's return of the Cherokee National Capitol Building, the seat of tribal courts and government before 1907. In a brief but moving address, Principal Chief Wilma Mankiller acknowledged the complexity of the transition and observed, "The Cherokees have always been in search of Justice." Almost a decade later, Chadwick Smith at his inauguration as Chief again proclaimed the historic ties of the Cherokee people with the rule of law. Considering the tribe's role in the key Indian law cases *Cherokee Nation v. Georgia*, 30 U.S. (5 Pet.) 1 (1831), and *Worcester v. Georgia*, 31 U.S. (6 Pet.) 515 (1832), no tribe in American history has been more closely associated with courts and the court system.[1]

The establishment and operation of their own constitutional-based court system is an important chapter in this Native American legal drama. Because the book *Indian Justice* records one of the early trials under this new Cherokee legal system, it is a unique document in the history of American law and the evolution of Native jurisprudence. Originally published in the *New York Journal of Commerce* in April 1841, this detailed narrative of a Cherokee murder trial was recorded by John Howard Payne, the distinguished nineteenth-century literary and theatrical figure. An annotated version of these essays was published in 1933–34 with an introduction by Grant Foreman, a leading western lawyer and Indian historian of the era.

Best remembered today as the author of the song "Home Sweet Home," John Howard Payne briefly lived among the Cherokees before their removal from Georgia to the Indian Territory in the 1830s. Many of his articulate and sympathetic accounts of the Georgia-Cherokee conflict had already been published by 1840 when he came to the Cherokee Nation in what is present-day Oklahoma. He came as the invited guest of Chief John Ross, arriving on the heels of the infamous Cherokee Trail of Tears of 1838–39. Payne intended to publish a major Cherokee tribal history for which he was collecting data. Although the book was never completed, many of the papers he gathered are available to contemporary researchers at the Newberry Library in Chicago.[2]

At the turn of the century, the book's editor, Grant Foreman, a University of Michigan Law School graduate, came to Muskogee in the Indian Territory as attorney for the Dawes Commission allotment of tribal lands.[3] After a lucrative career as an Indian lands attorney, Foreman retired to become a full-time historian. Noted as a meticulous researcher in primary documents, Foreman uncovered this newspaper narrative of the trial while gathering materials on Indian Territory in the post-removal era.

The heart of *Indian Justice* is Payne's meticulously detailed account, including verbatim transcriptions, of the murder trial and events surrounding the conviction of Cherokee citizen Archilla Smith. The narrative centers on the trial in Tahlequah, Cherokee Nation, which begins on December 15, 1840, and climaxes with the execution of the defendant on January 1, 1841. In the conclusion of his published account of the trial, John Howard Payne describes his struggle to produce the document:

I have had more difficulty than anyone can imagine, who has never experienced the impediments to gathering any sort of information in such regions, and especially where it must be obtained through Indian languages. In the present case, I have had to procure translations throughout from both Cherokees and

Creeks; and to glean particulars from numberless sources, in addition to what I observed myself.

Almost as important as Payne's first-hand observations are Grant Foreman's introductory analysis and insightful notes. As both an attorney and Indian historian, Foreman brings a unique perspective to the people and the time. He highlights the social and political conflicts as well as the personalities that dominate the Cherokee Nation and this murder trial. Both Payne and Foreman have a decidedly pro-Ross perspective in a time that verged on intense tribal civil war. In many ways, this criminal case mirrors the unsettled peace that followed the 1839 union of the Eastern and Old Settler Cherokees. The book, however, focuses upon the Cherokee world shown to outsiders and ignores the inner, back-country, and traditional tribal ways. Payne lacked the experience or advisors to help him look deeply beneath the surface of Anglo-Saxon legal forms.

At the time of the Archilla Smith trial, the Cherokee Nation had undertaken a unique experiment in social and legal acculturation—a blending of ancient Cherokee legal traditions with a written Anglo-based constitutional system.[4] In 1808 this southeastern tribe adopted their first written law. It sought to replace the clan revenge system for regulation of homicide with a court trial based on English and American concepts.[5] By 1840, when Payne was recording this trial, the new system had been in operation long enough for Cherokee tribal traditions to merge into the formality of ancient Anglo-Saxon ways. While Payne and Foreman provide significant and detailed views of the outward legal procedures and the specific facts and formal arguments from this trial, much of the surviving Indianness of the proceedings is missed. Unfortunately, much of the Cherokee perspective is missing from their accounts.

The unique intermingling of newly written Anglo-based law and the ancient spiritual culture that dominated Cherokee law is not generally reflected in Payne's account. He does note, however, the temptation to return to the old clan revenge system as well as the court's discussion of the former system. For example, Payne describes the heavy use of tobacco in the courtroom. He apparently does not recognize or understand the ritual, spiritual, and magical uses of treated smoke in a legal setting.

As late as the mid-1960s, Cherokee ethnologists Jack and Anna Kilpatrick discovered the survival of the use of magical incantations (idi: gawe; sdi) "to remake tobacco to weary judges, to create indecision in juries, to raise dissension in the prosecution team and to addle witnesses."[6] Specific formulas reported by the Kilpatricks included those for minor crimes and for homicides and to assist prisoners in escape, aid fugitives from the law, and protect peace officers. The process of acquiring spiritual help in the courtroom was, in fact, a long and complex one with roots in the mystical mind of the Cherokee. This was not apparent to John Howard Payne or later non-Indian court observers such as George Foster, author of a similar report in the 1890s.[7] And yet, reading *Indian Justice*, a contemporary student of tribal law and history can see the internal struggle at the heart of Cherokee cultural uniqueness. The ambivalence of a society at a historic crossroads is clearly established in Payne's narrative.

A final observation should be noted. *Indian Justice* is a chapter in the Cherokee experience. Native justice in the nineteenth century was tribal-specific and uniquely focused upon individual cultures and traditions. It would be misleading to assume that other tribes, even close geographical neighbors, followed similar patterns of justice and courtroom behavior. There was little traditional, general "Indian law" that crossed tribal ways.[8] The Cherokee and the Sioux and the Creek and the Cheyenne often dealt with crimes such as murder in very different ways. These Indian ways, which best served Native people, were often found unacceptable by non-Indian society. The 1883 case of *Ex Parte Crow Dog*, 107 U.S. 556 (1883), ultimately produced the Major Crimes Act, dictating a federal punishment rather than traditional tribal criminal jurisprudence.[9] The U.S. Congress, in reaction to *Crow Dog*, was shocked that the Sioux did not execute the guilty party but required a murderer to support the family of his victim.

The Cherokees, unlike many other tribes, held on to their new system of justice until the end of the century. The so-called Five Civilized Tribes, including the Cherokees, continued to follow the "borrowed system," much like that described by John Howard Payne, until 1898. At that time their tribal courts were abolished by the Curtis Act.[10] Today the Cherokees, like all other federally recognized Indian tribes, no longer have tribal jurisdiction to punish homicide.[11] *Indian Justice* is the fascinating legal story of a unique time in the evolution of Native jurisprudence when the Cherokees were struggling to achieve a working relationship between their traditional values and a newly borrowed white-based legal system. As Grant Foreman concluded:

[John Howard Payne] has given us a remarkable picture of a court room scene in which the Indian actors are endeavoring with substantial success to try an important case according to laws and procedures and rules of evidence with which they were not familiar; and [to] apply . . . principles of justice and reason borrowed from the white man's body of laws. But throughout is discernable their own shrewd sense of justice.

The reissue of *Indian Justice* is particularly appropriate at this time when what Grant Foreman called the Indian's "own shrewd sense of justice" is being seriously tested in the courts of the United States. John Howard Payne's document is an affirmation of tribal courts' historic fairness in the protection of basic human rights. The Cherokees at the beginning of the twenty-first century are once again operating their own court system with a narrower jurisdiction but continuing, as Chief Mankiller noted, "in search of justice."

RENNARD STRICKLAND

September 2001

NOTES

1. For a more complete discussion of the identification of the Cherokees with law, see "To Do the Right Thing: Reaffirming Indian Traditions of Justice Under Law," in Rennard Strickland, *Tonto's Revenge: Reflections on American Indian Culture and Policy* (Albuquerque: Univ. of New Mexico Press, 1997), 77–84.

2. For a more detailed biographical sketch see Grant Foreman, "John Howard Payne and the Cherokee Indians," *American Historical Review* 37 (July 1932): 723–30.

3. Excellent background and biographical information can be found in Edward E. Dale, "A Dedication to the Memory of Grant Foreman, 1869–1953," *Arizona and the*

West 6 (winter 1964): 271–74; and J. Stanley Clark, "Grant Foreman," *Chronicles of Oklahoma* 31 (August 1953): 226–42.

4. For more extensive development of this analysis, see Rennard Strickland, *Fire and the Spirits: Cherokee Law from Clan to Court* (Norman: Univ. of Oklahoma Press, 1975).

5. For additional analysis of Cherokee legal, cultural, and social change, see John Phillip Reid, *A Better Kind of Hatchet: Law, Trade and Diplomacy in the Cherokee Nation During the Early Years of Contact* (University Park: Pennsylvania State Univ. Press, 1976); John Phillip Reid, *A Law of Blood: Primitive Law of the Cherokee Nation* (New York: New York Univ. Press, 1970); and Theda Perdue, *Cherokee Women: Gender and Culture Change, 1700–1835* (Lincoln: Univ. of Nebraska Press, 1998).

6. See, generally, Jack Frederick Kilpatrick and Anna Gritts Kilpatrick, *Run Toward the Nightland: Magic of the Oklahoma Cherokees* (Dallas: Southern Methodist Univ. Press, 1968).

7. George Foster, "A Legal Episode in the Cherokee Nation," *Green Bag* 4 (1892), 486–90. For information on other Cherokee court cases, see Grant Foreman, "The Trial of Stand Watie," *Chronicles of Oklahoma* 12 (September 1934): 305–39; and Jack Kilpatrick and Anna G. Kilpatrick, "Record of a North Carolina Cherokee Township Trial, 1862," *Southern Indian Studies* 16 (1964).

8. For a comparative approach to tribal legal systems, see Rennard Strickland, "Wolf Warriors and Turtle Kings: American Indian Law Before the Blue Coats," *University of Washington Law Review* 72 (1997): 1043.

9. See Rennard Strickland's analysis of *Ex Parte Crow Dog*, 109 U.S. 557 (1883) in *The Oxford Companion to the Supreme Court of the United States*, ed. Kermit L. Hall (New York: Oxford Univ. Press, 1992).

10. 1898 Curtis Act, Act of June 28, 1898, Ch. 517, 30 Stat 495.

11. For a more detailed analysis of contemporary tribal jurisdiction and federal court jurisprudence, see *Handbook of Federal Indian Law*, ed. Rennard Strickland and Felix S. Cohen (Charlottesville: Michie Bobbs-Merrill Law Publishers, 1982).

INTRODUCTION

The driving of the Indians from the Southern States to the present Oklahoma, in its larger aspect covering the period from 1830 to 1840, was an undertaking of absorbing interest to the whole country. The wrongs to which these Indians were subjected and the interesting experiment of transporting whole tribes bodily from their ancestral domain to the West where they were to carve new homes out of the wilderness, resulted in many contemporary accounts in the press, and a few more serious efforts by writers making some claims to scholarship. Of the latter one of the most interesting, just, and sympathetic was John Howard Payne, who engaged in a serious study of the Cherokee Indians with a view to writing their history. It is somewhat of a coincidence that his visit to the Indians following their removal west was only a few years after the visit of his old friend Washington Irving to the same section of what is now Oklahoma. Their motives and accomplishments, however, were vastly different. Irving came to this country wholly by chance, as a lark,[1] and while his experi-

---

[1]Irving was traveling with some friends on Lake Erie when they

ence inspired the classic *A Tour on the Prairies*, and while he was more celebrated as a writer, he contributed little to our knowledge of the Indians of Oklahoma. Payne, however, was profoundly interested in the Cherokee Indians and his industry produced material that, when made available, will enable us to know much more about them than we do now.

John Howard Payne was born in New York City June 9, 1792. He passed his early boyhood at East Hampton, Long Island, and studied elocution in Boston where he also took part when very young in amateur theatricals. To remove him from stage influence he was placed in the counting house of his late brother's firm in New York City, but this precocious youth managed while only fourteen years old to edit and publish a small paper, the *The Thespian Mirror* (1805–6) of which files still exist. Mr. Coleman manager of the *Evening Post* becoming interested in

met Henry L. Ellsworth of Hartford, Connecticut, who was on his way to Fort Gibson to join other members of a commission to which they had recently been appointed: there they were to perform duties assigned them in connection with the Indians emigrating to the western country. Mr. Ellsworth invited Irving and his friends to join him on his journey to the West and they gladly accepted. They arrived at Fort Gibson October 8, 1832, and soon departed for a tour of the country to the west described by Irving in his *Tour on the Prairies*. They returned to Fort Gibson a month later; a day or two after, Mr. Irving descended the Arkansas River on his way to Washington (Irving, Pierre M., *The Life and Letters of Washington Irving*, III, 34; Latrobe, Charles Joseph, *The Rambler in North America*, I, 103; Trent, William P. and George S. Hellman, *The Journals of Washington Irving*, the Bibliophile Society, III, 101, ff.; Foreman, Grant, *Pioneer Days in the Early Southwest*, 85).

the lad, arranged for him to attend Union College, where he remained for two years, and edited an undergraduate publication, *The Pastime.*

His father's bankruptcy led young Payne to return to New York, and to take up the stage as a profession. At the age of seventeen he made his debut at the Park Theatre, New York, February 24, 1809, as *Young Norval,* in Home's *Douglas,* and achieved an immediate success, winning the title of "The American Roscius." The next year he played leading parts in Hamlet and in 1813 he visited England and, meeting with equal success in the part of *Young Norval* in London and other cities, established himself in that country as an actor, playwright, and manager.

He frequently appeared in Drury Lane Theatre, but his regular appearance as an actor ceased in 1814, when he turned his attention to the adaptation of plays from the French. Subsequently he produced his tragedy, *Brutus; or the Fall of Tarquin,* which was produced with Edmund Kean in the principal part at the Drury Lane Theatre. The opera *Clari; or the Maid of Milan,* by Payne and Sir Henry Bishop was produced at the Covent Garden Theatre May 8, 1823. It contained Payne's famous song "Home Sweet Home" which was sung by Miss M. Tree; the air was an adaptation by Sir Henry of a similar theme Payne had heard in Italy.[2]

---

[2]*Harper's Encyclopaedia of United States History.* VII, 95; Nel-

Payne had a disastrous experience as manager of Saddlerswell Theatre in London and in order to escape imprisonment for debt he went to Paris. There, in 1823, he was joined by his friend Washington Irving, six years older than he, and for some time they occupied an apartment together. They had many interesting friends in common, including Walter Scott, Tom Moore, and Charles Lamb; but of greater interest than any of these was Mary Wollstonecraft Shelley, the widow of the poet, with whom there began a romance as early as 1824. From that time Payne unsuccessfully wooed the heart of this beautiful and captivating young widow, with whom he kept up a correspondence for six or seven years. Learning at last that she was using him as a foil to promote her siege of his friend, the fascinating Washington Irving, he finally abandoned his fruitless quest.[3]

Payne returned to the United States in 1832 and three years later we find him traveling through the South in search of material he hoped to use in

son's *Encyclopaedia*, IX, 264: George Grove, *A Dictionary of Music and Musicians*, I, 245, 745.

[3]*The Romance of Mary W. Shelley, John Howard Payne, and Washington Irving*, The Biblophile Society, Boston, 1907. After Payne's return to the United States he resided in Washington for some time and contributed to the *Democratic Review* and other periodicals. In 1842 he was appointed U. S. consul at Tunis, where he resided until his death in 1852. His body was disinterred there in 1883 and reburied in Washington.

writing about that section of the country. By chance he came in contact with the Indians: "In traveling through Georgia, I of course, heard frequent mention of Cherokees; but I took little heed of what I heard. I considered the Cherokees as they had been represented, as but the miserable remnant of a broken race given up to all sorts of degradations; and I thought the sooner they could be transported beyond the bounds of civilization, the better for the world. Accident, however, brought me to some very different views of the question. I inquired more thoroughly. I determined to judge them with my own eyes. I purchased a horse, traversed the forests alone, and went among them.

"Still I was perplexed; I was desirous of seeing the headmen of the tribe; I was particularly desirous of seeing John Ross. Some Georgians told me I ought not to see him; that he was a selfish, and a sordid, and a silent man, in whom I should take no interest, from whom I should obtain no information. At one moment I had turned aside from my purpose, and was proceeding homeward. But I felt as if my errand would be a fruitless one if I went away. So little instructed, I changed my course, and traveled the wilderness for three days to the abode of Mr. Ross.

"I found Mr. Ross a different man, in every respect, from what I had heard him represented to be. His person is of middle size, rather under than over;

his age is about five and forty; he is mild, intelligent, and entirely unaffected. I told him my object. He received me with cordiality. He said he regretted that he had only a log cabin of but one room to invite me to, but he would make no apologies."[4] Payne remained several weeks at the home of the Chief making observations and notes on the condition and history of the Indians. He was permitted to copy documents of historical importance and he compiled a large mass of interesting material about the tribe which he planned to use in writing their history.[5] He prepared for the press a succinct statement of the case of the Indians and their oppression by the whites, the first time perhaps that a man of his talents had performed this service for them.[6] His account included a most interesting description of the

---

[4]*U.S. Senate Document* No. 120, p. 573, Twenty-fifth Congress, second session. Ross's comfortable plantation on the Coosa River in Georgia had been seized by the authorities of that state, who bestowed it on the fortunate drawer in a lottery set up by the state to confiscate the valuable improvements of the Cherokee Indians. The Chief and his family were driven out and sought refuge in Tennessee in a log cabin.

[5]This material was not used, however, for Payne never wrote his history. After his death this collection was disposed of and is now to be seen in the *Ayer Collection* in the Newberry Library in Chicago. The editor recently learned that a collection of Payne material had been advertised for sale twenty or thirty years ago by Maggs Brothers of London. Thinking this might be some new material that he had not seen, he inquired of these dealers about it; and following up their information he finally traced it into the Newberry Library, it being the same collection that he had examined there on several occasions.

[6]*U.S. Senate Document* No. 120, p. 573, Twenty-fifth Congress, second session.

Cherokee Indians come to confer with their chief at his home in Tennessee, and gather at the council grounds nearby to consider a proposed treaty.

Payne's interest in the Indians inspired several graphic written accounts of what he saw on that journey. Among them was a long description of the Creek Indians contained in a letter to his sister, now recognized by historians and ethnologists as an important contribution to their fields of study.[7] During his stay at the home of Chief Ross his sympathy for the Indians involved him in serious difficulties. The chief's home was broken into by a company of the Georgia guard, who seized Payne's papers without legal process of any kind, carried him and his host across the line into Georgia, and incarcerated them in prison for more than a week. On their release Payne was ordered out of the country. To this experience we are indebted for another interesting paper giving a picture of the people and times associated with that high-handed outrage.[8]

---

[7]This narrative was a description of an aboriginal festival known as the green corn dance witnessed by Payne in the Tukabahchee town of the Creek Nation. The ritual was described by him in one of his most polished and graphic efforts, and presents that phase of the life of the Creek Indians, together with its historical associations, in a most interesting manner. This paper was printed in *The Continental Monthly*, (1862) Vol. I, 17–29. It was more recently republished with an introduction and footnotes by Dr. John R. Swanton, in *Chronicles of Oklahoma*, X, 170–195.

[8]*Knoxville (Tenn.) Register*, December 2, 1835; *Georgia Constitutionalist*, December 24, 1835; Batty, George A., *A History of Rome*

After this experience among the Cherokee people, Payne retained a lively interest in their affairs; during the next few years he conferred with their leading men when they visited Washington and other places in the East and kept up a correspondence with them. It was natural then that when the whole nation was driven west, his interest in their welfare and curiosity concerning the changes effected by emigration should have taken him where he could see them in their new home and observe them in the process of readjustment to their new environment.

The great body of Cherokee Indians started on their westward march in the autumn of 1838. They reached their destination in the late winter and early spring,[9] and, though broken-spirited, impoverished,

and *Floyd County* [Georgia] (Atlanta), 1922, 55–74. This interesting and detailed account by Payne of the outrages to which he and Ross were subjected is an illuminating picture of the people, red and white, whom he met there. The invasion of Tennessee soil by the Georgians caused great excitement and resentment in the state of the former.

[9]Foreman, Grant, *Indian Removal, the Emigration of the Five Civilized Tribes;* ibid., *Indians and Pioneers.* Several thousand Cherokee had removed to the West prior to the enactment of the Indian Removal Bill in 1830. December 29, 1835, a small number of unauthorized Cherokee men of prominence were induced by representatives of the government to sign what was called a treaty, by which these men undertook to yield the lands of the tribe in the East and agree to remove to the West. Though this fraudulent document was repudiated by ninety per cent of the tribe, it was presented to the senate and ratified. A few thousand of the tribe then voluntarily removed, but as the remainder refused, soldiers were sent into their country in 1838; the Indians were made captives in their homes, herded into concentration camps and driven out of the country. The largest movement of these unhappy people occurred in

sick and reduced by many deaths, they at once began the construction of new homes. On July 12 an act of union between the new arrivals and the older residents and a new constitution were adopted. The next year, 1840, the first Cherokee council under the new constitution assembled at Tahlequah, the Cherokee capital.

During the session of this council Payne came to their new country and spent four months as the guest of Chief John Ross at his home in Park Hill. He came with the definite purpose of seeking more material for his intended history of Cherokee people. The result was that instead of attempting descriptions of mere frontier adventures, Payne set down instructive accounts of the red people with whom he came in contact. He wrote a number of interesting papers for the press and his friends in the East, including descriptions of the Indians in legislative council that it is hoped to bring to light, so that the industry he employed in recording his impressions and observations can be made available to present-day students.

The subjoined description by Payne of a Cherokee court trial is one of these. It readily will be rec-

---

the autumn of that year, when about thirteen thousand of them, in thirteen parties began their sad journey through Tennessee, Kentucky, southern Illinois, Missouri, and Arkansas into eastern Indian Territory. During the arrest, concentration and emigration of these people, about four thousand of them died.

ognized by historians and students as a valuable contribution to our knowledge of the Cherokee Indians. As a picture of an Indian people ninety years ago well on the road from a primitive life to a high state of civilization it stands alone. Except for the more comprehensive journal of Major Hitchcock written the next year,[10] there is no other contemporary description of the Cherokee people of that time comparable to it; and even Hitchcock's effort does not contain a more eye-filling picture of any one phase of Cherokee life.

Payne has given us not only what he says is the first complete account ever to be put in print of an Indian trial with its forms and speeches and judicial charges, but he has done more; he has written the first newspaper account of a court trial in Oklahoma and one of the best ever written in any state. Unprepared to witness a formal judicial proceeding in this remote Indian country, this veteran actor and playright found the stage set for one of the most dramatic scenes he had ever beheld, and with the intuition of his versatile mind, and the skill that came with his long training, he wrote that drama for others to see. He wrote not only the correspondent's detailed account of the essentials of the trail, but, unhampered by newspaper rules governing space and form, he

---

[10]Grant Foreman (Ed.) *A Traveler in Indian Territory. The Journal of Ethan Allen Hitchcock.*

sketched in sidelights and background and atmosphere without stint, so that the reader could see all the dramatic elements of the situation.

He has given us a remarkable picture of a court room scene in which the Indian actors are endeavoring with substantial success to try an important case according to laws and procedure and rules of evidence with which they were not familiar; and awkwardly to apply to the matter before them principles of justice and reason borrowed from the white man's body of laws. But throughout is discernable their own shrewd sense of justice and comprehension of the significance of the evidence against the defendant that determined his fate. And despite the bitter factional controversies then raging in the Cherokee Nation and the fact that the defendant belonged to the faction opposing the established government, the intention to give him a fair trial is manifest throughout. Both presiding judges showed themselves just and unprejudiced and disposed to protect the defendant in all his rights; the rulings and charge to the jury by Chief Justice Bushyhead stamp him as a man of intelligence and learning and judicial temperament whose death three years later was an incalculable loss to the Cherokee Nation.

This account was written in the most painstaking manner, and the great amount of labor and care employed by Payne and the difficulties surmounted by him are obvious. His assurance of the minute accuracy of his work must carry conviction to the reader, as his conscientious striving for a faithful portrayal of all he saw is evident throughout. The account appeared in two long installments in *The New York Journal of Commerce* for April 17 and April 29, 1841, and was never printed elsewhere so far as is known.

GRANT FOREMAN

I

THE CAPTURE OF ARCHILLA SMITH

Washington City, March 10, 1841.

Some time ago I wrote to you from the Cherokee Nation west of Arkansas. I have since returned to Washington City from that region. Events occurred there subsequently to the date of my last letter, which may be of some interest to your readers. I will relate them to you; and, especially, all the particulars of a trial for murder, which took place during my sojourn. As, probably, the first detail which was ever put in print of an Indian trial, with its forms and speeches and judicial charges, your readers may not be disposed to quarrel with its length; even though it extend over so much paper, as to render it necessary for me to divide it into two or three numbers.

The trial I allude to is that of Archilla Smith,[1]

[1]Archilla Smith emigrated to the west in 1837 with one of the parties that came more or less voluntarily after the execution of the treaty of removal. This party departed from Ross's Landing, now Chattanooga, Tennessee, March 3, 1837, traveled by steamboats and keel boats in tow and debarked on the north bank of the Arkansas River just above Fort Smith on the twenty-eighth of the month. The party, numbering 466, included the Ridge and Watie families and their friends. Dr. C. Lillybridge, who accompanied these Indians, kept an interesting diary of their experiences, which was published with introduction and footnotes by Grant Foreman in *The Mississippi Valley Historical Review,* September, 1931, XVIII, 232.

a Cherokee of note, who was among the signers of the
false treaty.[1]   Archilla Smith always had the character of a reckless and violent person. He was tall;—ex-
pert with the rifle and ready with the tomahawk and
knife;—and had been, it is said, in more brawls than
any Indian in the country.   When the United States
Agent arrived at Fort Gibson soon after the return of
the Principal Chief in October last, Archilla Smith
and some relatives and particular friends of his, against
most of whom charges were out either for robbery or
murder, banded themselves together, armed, near the
most frequented way from the interior of the nation to
the fort.   Archilla Smith was under an accusation of
having some months previously murdered a young man
by the name of John MacIntosh.   In his drunken
revels he would defy the power of the constituted authorities of his country. He and his associates kept the
whole neighborhood in alarm. At the same time Cherokees returning homeward with monies received at the
Fort from our government in payment for their posses-
sions east of the Mississippi, were assaulted as they
passed there, instances occurred, it is said, of lives being
taken; and yet more of passengers being deprived of all
they had about them; even to their clothes.

Archilla Smith had heard that there was a warrant out against him from the Cherokee courts; but he

---

[1] "The false treaty" was the term used to indicate the notor-
iously fraudulent document known as the Cherokee treaty of 1835.

openly proclaimed that he would not be taken, and never went about without his weapons and friends well armed. One day, from the cabin where he was, he sent an Indian boy out twice in succession for drink. Each time, as he took the cup, part of the liquor fell upon the ground. On the second spilling, he gazed at the cup, and stood for a moment as if stupified. "I shall be taken," exclaimed he;—and handing his weapons to the boy, desired him to remove them, lest he should do the mischief he had threatened. After this, he appears to have fallen asleep and to have been startled up by the tramp of horses. At that instant the door was burst open, and some twenty Indians sprang in. Archilla Smith had already seized a gun. One person struck him by the side of the head, collared and stripped him and jerked away the gun. Two rifles were leveled at him. He cried for quarter. With some difficulty the Indian sheriff restrained his men from firing. Archilla Smith gave himself up; and with him the guard took into custody a young man by the name of William Webber, who, at the first alarm, made a move to hand Archilla Smith weapons to defend himself.

There are no prisons in the Cherokee country;[13] so a prisoner must always be watched by a guard at some

---

[13]As in the early days there were no prisons in the Cherokee country, the laws provided for summary punishment, which was usually inflicted by whipping except in the case of capital punishment. Later, however, punishments by fines and imprisonment were substituted.

private house; and, in order to incommode families as little as possible, a cavalcade of that sort changes its stopping place from cabin to cabin, seldom passing more than two or three days at any one. The entertainment is, of course, at the expense of the public treasury.

No sooner had the prisoners been housed for the night, than their friends scattered reports in every direction to provoke alarms. Some appeared to hope that the national authorities might be intimidated. On the same evening, near the Principal Chief's, an Indian pretending to be drunk, went singing around the log hut; and now and then he paused to raise the single war-hoop, which is given to proclaim the killing of one foe.

Several days elapsed before all was in readiness for the trial. Meanwhile, the prisoners were frequently transferred from hut to hut. One afternoon a number of wild looking armed men on horseback rode towards the abode of the Principal Chief. Before his gate they suddenly reined in their steeds. A voice cried to John Ross, who was sitting in the open central passage between the two parts of the hut, "Can we have water?" "Yes," was the answer, "but won't you alight?" A moment's pause ensued. A second person now spurred his horse in advance of the first and answered "Yes." The first speaker alighted and was followed by the others; but the second bustled through them all, and heading the party, they entered the Principal Chief's dwelling.

He who had taken the lead, thus, was Archilla

Smith. He wore red leggings;—a shabby green blanket
coat, descending to his heels. The other was William
Webber. Though prisoners, they had the air of captains
of the strange party. All were received alike and cour-
teously; all shook hands with the chief and his friends.
Chief Ross observed in an inquiring whisper to some
one as they went in, "Is it Archilla Smith?"

Said the prisoner to the Chief, in Cherokee, "How
are you?—It is sometime, now, since we met.—How
long?"

"Some years, I think."

"You and I are beginning to get into years. We
were both of us good looking once," remarked Archilla
Smith.

"The fairest flowers must wither as their season
passes," answered the Chief.

"You are fatter than when I saw you last," observed the prisoner.

"I am fatter than I was a short time ago, but not
so fat as I have been.—Have you been well?" said Chief
Ross.

"Yes," replied Archilla Smith, "but the men have
me; and they have some purpose in view, for which,
probably, they fancy there is cause."

A stir in the group, intermingled with careless gos-
sip, followed:—after which the prisoner, starting up
from his seat, exclaimed.

"I thought I would look in and see you. We must

continue our way, now; and I may journey on and on,
and may, perhaps, see you no more."

The whole band then re-mounted, and galloped away
to their place of safe keeping for the night."

A similar stop at the same place, when riding by
in the same manner, was made once again at Archilla
Smith's request, previous to his trial. On this occasion,
very little passed between him and the Principal Chief,
beyond the ordinary civilities. Archilla Smith conversed, however, sometime with a distant relation whom
he met there;—John Benge, a person of note in the
nation. He intimated to Benge that he did not know
why he was a prisoner. Benge told him he had understood it was for killing MacIntosh. He replied, Mac-
Intosh was a relation of his; and it was a very unlikely
story that he would kill a relation. He added that he
hoped he would not be hurried off, but have a fair hearing and all his friends present. He was answered that
his trial would be a fair one, and that he might call any
witness he chose, to speak for him. He asked who the
prosecutor was. He was told it was the High-Sheriff,
who, by law, was bound to bring all such cases to justice. He asked whether the law was the same as that in

"Payne, who was a guest in the home of Chief Ross, was a
witness of this visit of Archilla Smith and his guard in the Ross
home. He described it in a long letter to John Watterston published
with introduction and footnotes by Grant Foreman in *The American
Historical Review*, July, 1932, XXXVII, 723; see also Grant Foreman, *Advancing the Frontier*, 320.

the old nation. He was told that it was pretty much the same; and that the Sheriff was obliged to seek and bring into court any witnesses in the nation, that he might think capable of doing him the least service, be they far away or near. He seemed desirous of learning the name of the Judge and the time fixed for his trial. John Benge conjectured it would be Looney Price, as the nearest at hand; but added, that the time for trial must depend upon arrangements not yet completed. At length it arrived, and the 15th of December, 1840, was

THE FIRST DAY OF TRIAL:

and the place fixed for it was the Council Ground,[15] which I have described to you in a former letter.

The court-house was a log hut, of about eighteen feet square, with a bare-ground floor, and a large fire place and chimney opposite the entrance door. On the right side of the entrance, there were benches of rough boards for the jury, and the witnesses and the Interpreters;—a chair for the judge, and a chair and table for the clerk. On the left side, was a similar bench against the wall, for the accused and his guard and his friends.

The accused had been guarded on the night previous in another hut of the same sort, upon the same ground.

---

[15]The council ground was afterward included within the grounds of the Cherokee capital in Tahlequah. In 1841, when the place was visited by Colonel Hitchcock, it contained a large open shed within which the council met, and a number of log houses with dirt floors in which the committees conferred and prepared their reports.

As I myself came thither, I saw him sitting on a chair, in his green blanket coat, before the front of this hut. His guard, in their wild, uncouth dresses, and grim arms, were standing or sitting all about;—some of them, ever with their eyes riveted on him; but all, both prisoner and guard, were in an air of perfect unconcern and *bon hommie,* though I fancied there was an expression of deeper thoughtfulness on the brow of the accused, than of the rest. William Webber, I ought to have before stated, had been set free, on giving assurances not to attempt the rescue of his friend.

At length, a summons came, and the accused was escorted to the court. Part of the guard remained outside of the door. Looney Price, one of the associate judges of the Cherokee Supreme Court, presided. Isaac Bushyhead appeared as counsel for the nation. Stand Watie[16] (a brother of the late Elias Boudinot)[17] and

---

[16]Stand Watie (native name *De gata ga,* conveying the meaning that two persons are standing together so closely united in sympathy as to form but one human body). A noted Cherokee Indian, son of Uweti and half brother of Elias Boudinot, and after his death a leader of the party which had signed the removal treaty of New Echota. On the outbreak of the Civil War he and his party were the first to ally themselves with the South, and he was given command of one of two Cherokee regiments which had joined the Confederate forces and participated in the battle of Pea Ridge and in other actions. Later he led his regiment back to Indian Territory, and in conjunction with Confederate sympathizers from other tribes laid waste the fields and destroyed the property of the Indians who espoused the Federal cause. In revenge for the death of his brother he burned the house of John Ross, the head chief. He is further noted as one of the principal authorities for the legends and other

William Holt, appeared as agent, or counsel, for the accused. Both of these last were of the same politics with Archilla Smith, and had signed, as he had, the false treaty.

Judge Price informed the accused that a verdict would be pronounced upon his case by twelve of his countrymen, who were to be chosen from the following list of twenty four:

STEPHEN FOREMAN,   MOSES PARRIS,

ELIJAH HICKS,   JOHN NAVE,

---

material collected by Schoolcraft among the Cherokee (F. W. Hodge, (ed) *Handbook of the American Indians*) (Smithsonian Institution, Bureau of American Ethnology, Bulletin 30) II, 634.

[17]Elias Boudinot (native name *Galagi na,* 'male deer' or 'turkey'). A Cherokee Indian, educated in the foreign mission school at Cornwall, Connecticut, founded by the American Board of Commissioners for Foreign Missions, which he entered with two other Cherokee youths in 1818 at the instance of the philanthropist whose name he was allowed to adopt. In 1827 the Cherokee council formally resolved to establish a national paper, and the following year the *Cherokee Phoenix* appeared under Boudinot's editorship. After a precarious existence of a few years, however, the paper was discontinued and not resumed until after the removal of the Cherokee to Indian Territory, when its place was finally taken by the *Cherokee Advocate,* established in 1844. In 1843 Boudinot wrote "Poor Sarah; or the Indian Woman," in Cherokee characters, published at New Echota by the United Brethren's Missionary Society, another edition of which was printed at Park Hill in 1843; and from 1828 to the time of his death he was joint translator with Rev. S. A. Worcester of a number of the Gospels, some of which passed through several editions. Boudinot joined an insignificant minority of his people in support of the Ridge treaty and the subsequent treaty of New Echota. . . For that he was killed June 22, although not with the knowledge or connivance of the tribal officers (*Handbook of the American Indians, ibid.,* I, 162).

CHARLES THOMPSON,	A-LA-NE-TAH,
JAMES SU-WE-CUL-LAH,	TERRAPIN-HEAD,
THOMAS WOLF,	THOMAS TAYLOR,
THOMAS TERRILLE,	THOMAS CANDY,
ANDERSON LOWREY,	HORSE-FLY
JEFFERSON HAIR,	JOHN BOSTON,
GEORGE PARRIS,	ROBERT NEEF,
JOSIAH WICKED,	SHARP,
PARTRIDGE McELMORE,	SAMUEL BELL,
GEORGE DICK,	THOMAS RIDER.

From these, the Judge said the accused might reject twelve without assigning any reasons; but if he had objections to any, after having thrown out twelve, his objections must be stated and decided upon by the court. The accused then objected to the following persons:

ELIJAH HICKS,	PARTRIDGE McELMORE,
MOSES PARRIS,	TERRAPIN-HEAD,
JOHN NAVE,	THOMAS CANDY,
CHARLES THOMPSON,	HORSE-FLY,
JEFFERSON HAIR,	JOHN BOSTON,
GEORGE PARRIS,	ROBERT NEEF.

The remaining twelve being then empannelled as a jury, stood thus:

STEPHEN FOREMAN,¹⁸ (a native preacher),* Foreman,

JAMES SU-WE-CUL-LA,	ANDERSON LOWREY,
THOMAS TERRILLE,	GEORGE DICK,
JOSIAH WICKED,	THOMAS TAYLOR,
A-LA-NE-TAH,	SAMUEL BELL,
SHARP,	THOMAS RIDER.
THOMAS WOLF,	

Their names being called over, the following oath

---

*Educated, I believe, at Princeton, New Jersey.

¹⁸Stephen Foreman was the son of a Scotchman and a Cherokee mother. His father dying while he was a young boy he was thrown on his own resources. By his own industry and the encouragement of his friends he secured some education in his youth and in his eighteenth year Rev. S. A. Worcester instructed him. He then attended college at Richmond, Virginia, after which he completed his education at Union and Princeton Theological Seminaries, and was then licensed by the Presbyterian board to preach among his people. For many years he was associated with the Rev. S. A. Worcester and during their lives they translated the New Testament from the English into Cherokee. Mr. Foreman was conductor of one of the parties of Cherokee emigrants that arrived in their new home February 27, 1839, numbering on their arrival 921. During his lifetime he filled in turn nearly every office in his tribe but that of chief, but he was especially interested in religion and education, and was the first superintendent of public schools ever appointed in the Cherokee Nation. At his personal expense of about $800 he erected a little church at Park Hill in which he preached. He died November 20, 1881, at Park Hill.

Hitchcock said: "I remained in Mr. Worcester's last night and attended a Cherokee monthly meeting for prayer. The service was conducted in both English and Cherokee. Mr. Foreman a Cherokee engaged in translating the bible into Cherokee, made an excellent prayer in English. It was perfectly appropriate—simple and natural

was administered to them by the Judge; who first bade them hold up their right hands:

"You and each of you, do solemnly swear that you will well and truly try the case which is now to be submitted to you, and left to your decision by the Court, in the case of the Cherokee Nation against Archilla Smith, on charge of murder and true verdict give, according to evidence; so help you God!"

The kiss to the Bible was given, as in the Courts of the United States.

The agents for the accused now observed that there was a material witness in his favor who was not present; and they desired that the trial might not be permitted to commence, until he could be brought. His name was John Young, and he lived some miles off.

Judge Price ordered the Sheriff immediately to go in pursuit of John Young, and to produce him, and the court was adjourned until the morning of the 10th of December, 1840,

THE SECOND DAY OF TRIAL,

when the Sheriff announced that John Young was in attendance.

---

and earnest. The Language pure English, entirely free from border defects. I have often had occasion to notice that the English in half-breeds is free from many prominent defects among our border people, West and South. It may be owing to the influence of the missionaries who are better instructed themselves. There may have been 25 or 30 people present last evening" (Hitchcock, 51).

The accused now answering that he was ready for his trial, the warrant under which he was apprehended, was read to him. (This simple document takes the place among the Cherokees, of the more elaborate "indictment" in our courts.) It was worded as follows:

CHEROKEE NATION,
Salisaw District. }

To any lawful officer,
Greeting:

Robert Brown, *High Sheriff of Salisaw District,*

You are hereby commanded to take the body of Archilla Smith, if to be found within your bounds, and him safely keep; and bring him before the Circuit Judge, or any one of the Judges of the Supreme Court, then and there to answer the charge of murder alleged against him, for taking the life of John MacIntosh, late in the fall of 1839, or early in the winter:

Fail not under penalty of the law in such cases provided.

Given under my hand November 11th, 1840.

Prosecuting Attorney   DAVID CARTER,

ISAAC BUSHYHEAD.   District Judge.

The accused was asked if he was guilty or not guilty of the crime against him.

He answered, "I am not guilty of the charge alleged."

The counsel for the nation Isaac Bushyhead,[19] now observed that he would produce evidence to prove the guilt of the accused; and the jury would have it in their power to form their conclusions, unguided by him. All he desired was unbiased justice; and he would therefore proceed to the examination without further comment.

Judge Price remarked that it would be proper to note the evidence in the case with great care. It had better be carefully written down in English; and great heed must be taken in translating it, neither to over-state nor under-state the slightest particular.

The clerk of the court and the foreman of the jury now prepared papers and pens; and all being in readiness, orders were given to call in the first witness. This was a Cherokee by the name of Gay-Nu-Gay.

When the judge rose to administer the oath, a juror asked if Gay-Nu-Gay knew what an oath was.

The counsel for the nation asked Gay-Nu-Gay if he understood that in taking an oath, he insured to himself a double punishment should he not tell the truth concerning the subject on which he was summoned;—in this world he would be severely chastised under the law,

---

[19]Isaac Bushyhead, a brother of the Rev. Jesse Bushyhead, was clerk of the Cherokee council the next year. On August 7, 1843, he was killed by enemies of the newly established Cherokee government, who tried to break up the first general election under the new constitution.

and despised by all his fellow-men; and in the world to
come his sufferings would be endless.

Gay-Nu-Gay replied that he knew he must tell
the truth and that he meant to tell it.   He was desired
to hold up his right hand, and the oath was administered.

Gay-Nu-Gay then declared:

"I and Archilla Smith were in a Creek camp,"
(meaning a slight structure thrown up by itinerant Creek
Indians who have taken shelter among the Cherokees,
for their temporary abode;) and John MacIntosh was
at Peter's house making a great deal of noise, and
saying he was much of a man.   A Creek man was
standing near the camp, holding Archilla Smith's
horse.   MacIntosh rode up against the bridle held by
the Creek and pulled him away.   He did so several
times, and then rode up against the camp, and he, or
his horse knocked off some boards, Archilla Smith
then got up and said he did not like that, and went out,—
at the same time unbuttoning his coat and pulling out
his knife.   Immediately MacIntosh made at him and
Archilla Smith then struck at MacIntosh with his
knife, and missed him several times, holding him by the

---

[20]Several hundred Creek Indians had fled to the Cherokee country to escape the persecutions of the white people and a number of
them intermarried in that tribe.   They later emigrated with them
and the Cherokee permitted them to settle in their country and be
amalgamated in their tribe.   This may have been a settlement of
such Creek Indians or of stragglers who had stopped in the Cherokee country on the way to their own.

coat. Then MacIntosh beat Archilla Smith with his fist. There was a good deal of noise, as if they were fighting; but it was dark; I could not see. Afterwards MacIntosh rode off in a gallop; and then his horse seemed to trot. Archilla Smith pretty soon returned, having his knife in his hand. After this we went to Peter's."

The cross-examination now began; but I regret much that I omitted to obtain upon the spot a memorandum of by whom the respective questions were asked. The whole passed in Cherokee and sometimes Creek; and the translation of the testimony which was written down in open Court merely notes the cross examination generally as question and answer, without specifying the questions asked by the Counsel for the accused. I believe, however, that the greater part of the interrogatories came from Stand Watie, not only in the instance of this witness but of all the rest. The following is the cross-questioning of Gay-Nu-Gay.

Question. "What time in the day was it, when this affair took place?"

Answer. "Not quite dark."

Question. "When Archilla Smith returned, how did his knife look?"

Answer. "I could not tell; for it was then dark."

Question. "How long after this before you all went to Peter's?"

Answer. "Some time afterwards."

Question. "Did you see MacIntosh on your way to Peter's?"

Answer. "Yes; he was lying near where we went along. His horse was standing by him. We supposed he was asleep."

Question. "What time did you find out he was dead?"

Answer. "Not until the next day."

Question. "Who went with you to Peter's?"

Answer. "Archilla Smith and two others; four of us in all."

II

It was now suggested that the Court be adjourned until the next morning at nine; and that, in the meantime, as some Creek testimony was to be produced, interpreters should be obtained. So the Court adjourned.

One point throughout this day's trial,—and indeed, all those which followed, must not be forgotten. There was no appearance of bitter feeling on either side. The accused and the judge and jury and spectators, all seemed in the best of humor with one another. The accused smoked much of the time; and his judge, and most of his jury, every now and then would get up and go across the log-court to him with "Arley, lend me your pipe;" and receive his pipe from his mouth (as is the Indian custom); and revel in the loan of a five minutes' smoke.[21]

---

[21]Colonel Hitchcock the next year described the appearance of the Cherokees in council: "One large-sized man over 50 dressed in an overcoat with large pockets, divested his head of a turban-like kerchief and advanced to the centre of the room, bowed profoundly to the speaker (all who had made regular speeches stood in the middle of the floor) and made some jocular remark I judge, as the reverend counselors all laughed. He then began his speech, his right hand thrust into his right coat pocket, a long pipe stem proceeding from the pocket extending along his arm to his elbow; with his left hand he made graceful gestures from time to time until he became excited and then both hands were employed in gesture, his person for the most part erect or but slightly bending forward" (Grant Foreman, *A Traveler in Indian Territory, The Journal of Ethan Allen Hitchcock*, 59).

The wife and handsome young daughter of the accused attended; and sat much of the time outside of the door; and frequently went to an open window and looked into the court room to listen. Some of the time, his aunt and others of his female relations were present. His three young sons, one a boy about ten,—the others about twelve and fifteen, were in the court room nearly all the time, and often sat by their father's side.

THIRD DAY OF TRIAL

When Nicholous was called into court and sworn.

"I was not there when the affray took place. What I know was told to me."

Counsel for the Nation. "You may stand aside."

John (a Creek) was called; and Horse-Fly, as Principal Interpreter; and John Smith and Ta-She-E-Tee as his assistants, were summoned to appear.

John, the Creek, was questioned as to his idea of an oath; and its responsibilities were explained to him. He was then duly sworn:

"The sun was low, and they were drinking at the camp. Archilla Smith and a Creek man were talking in the camp. MacIntosh came up whooping and telling what a man he was, and what he could do—I was holding Archilla Smith's horse. Archilla Smith took hold of the bridle of MacIntosh's horse and stabbed MacIntosh."

The accused here rose and asked, "Have I the privilege to speak?"

The Judge not immediately replying, the counsel for nation got up and observed: "You have the privilege to speak. You have the still further privilege that, if you suppose the agents already employed to plead your cause are not sufficient, you may employ any other to assist them."

The accused answered, "All I wanted was to know whether I had the privilege to speak."

The cross examination of John, the Creek now proceeded; and principally from Stand Watie; although, as I before explained, I am unable to particularize the questions which he or any other asked.

Question. "Who commenced the difficulty?"

Answer. "MacIntosh, by whooping."

Question. "Did MacIntosh make any threats against Archilla Smith while whooping?"

Answer. "No."

Question. "Was MacIntosh on his horse?"

Answer. "Yes."

Question. "Did he fall off his horse near there?"

Answer. "He went off."

Question. "How far did MacIntosh go before he fell off his horse?"

Answer. "Before he got to a house that was near there."

Question. "How long before MacIntosh was stabbed, did the witness see him?"

Answer. "The same night it was done."

Question. "Had he been stabbed with a knife?"

Answer. "Yes."

Question. "How often had he been stabbed?"

Answer. "But once."

Question. "Was it soon after dark that Archilla Smith stabbed MacIntosh?"

Answer. "Yes."

Question. "What did Archilla Smith do after he stabbed MacIntosh?"

Answer. "He went away soon after."

Question. "Was MacIntosh buried the next day?"

Answer. "I was not at the burying."

Question. "Did this affray take place on Caney,²² near Eagle's?"

Answer. "Yes."

Question. "Was it near Peter's house?"

Answer. "Yes. When they took up the body, they carried it to Peter's house."

Question. "Was MacIntosh killed, as mentioned, late in the fall, or first of the winter?"

Answer. "In the fall."

Question. "Were you acquainted with MacIntosh before this?"

---

²²Caney Creek flows into the Illinois River from the northeast about ten miles southeast of Tahlequah.

Answer. "I had seen him once or twice."

Question. "Had you heard his name?"

Answer. "Yes, it was Ah-Kungh-Yah-Shee, and in English, MacIntosh."

Question. "Were you acquainted with Archilla Smith before this?"

Answer. "Yes, I knew him and I knew his name."

Question. "Is this prisoner Archilla Smith?" (pointing to Archilla Smith.)

Answer. "Yes."

Question. "When MacIntosh went off, did you see him fall off?"

Answer. "No."

Question. "How long after Archilla Smith went away, before you saw MacIntosh?"

Answer. "Not long. It was dark."

Question. "Was the body taken away that night?"

Answer. "Yes."

Question. "Did you examine MacIntosh?"

Answer. "Yes; there was a light there."

Question. "When MacIntosh rode off, did he go fast or slow?"

Answer. "Slow."

Question. "Do you know anything about the commencement of the affray?"

Answer. "No—excepting what I have already stated."

Question. "Did MacIntosh make the horse break away from you?"

Answer. "Yes."

Question. "Did MacIntosh have a switch or a club?"

Answer. "A switch."

Question. "At the time MacIntosh was killed, were they drinking?"

Answer. "Yes; four persons; besides the man that was killed."

Question. "Did you ever get drunk?"

Answer. "I drink, but not so as to get drunk."

Question. "When the affair took place, did Archilla Smith and the others have whiskey?"

Answer. "Yes. Archilla Smith had some in a bottle."

Question. "Did you drink any with them?"

Answer. "Yes, about five drams," (*Here* **Stand** Watie *repeated the answer and looked* **round** *with a significant smile.*)

Question. "You were pretty drunk, I suppose?"

Answer. "Not much. I did not drink much. I was sick."

Question. "Had you drunk any before **Archilla** Smith came with whiskey?"

Answer. "No."

Question. "Was Soldier and (another **person**— the name not recollected)—drunk?"

Answer. "No. None but the man that was whooping." (Meaning MacIntosh.)

Sub-Be-Go, another Creek, was next called, and duly sworn.

"MacIntosh whooped and then came up, riding about and then would go off and come again. A young man would whoop and MacIntosh would return. He did so two or three times. Then Archilla Smith went out and caught his horse by the bridle. I could not tell what was done, but I heard the lick very distinctly. MacIntosh then went off towards a house close by and called several times and then ceased. When Archilla Smith and some others went off they did not go by the house. Archilla Smith is said to have come there the next morning. I did not see him. I know nothing more."

Sub-Be-Go, the Creek, was then cross-examined as follows:

Question. "How high was the sun when Archilla Smith came there?

Answer. "About sun down."

Question. "Was MacIntosh there when Archilla Smith came?"

Answer. "Not during the day. He came just after dark."

Question. "What time was it when Archilla Smith struck MacIntosh?"

Answer. *"Just after dark."*

Question. "Did you go where MacIntosh was calling?"

Answer. "No."

Question. "Did you see MacIntosh after he was struck?"

Answer. "Yes, the next morning."

Question. "Was MacIntosh dead when you saw him the next morning?"

Answer. "Yes."

Question. "Did you see any wound by a knife, or any thing, on his body?"

Answer. "No. He was already dressed and lying by the fire."

Question. "Was the corpse buried the same day you saw it?"

Answer. "Yes,—the same day,—late in the evening."

Question. "Did you see Archilla Smith have anything in his hand?"

Answer. "Yes, I saw him have a knife."

Question. "Were you acquainted with MacIntosh before this?

Answer. "No, I had not seen him before."

Question. "Did you know his name?"

Answer. "No."

Question. "Had you seen Archilla Smith before he struck MacIntosh?"

Answer. "Yes. I knew him."

Question. "Is this Archilla Smith sitting here?" (pointing at Archilla Smith.)

Answer. "Yes."

Question. "After Archilla Smith struck the lick how long after this was it that he struck him with the knife?"

Answer. "At the same time. The noise was caused by the lick with the knife."

Question. "Was it at your house that this was done?"

Answer. "Yes."

Question. "Was it dark, or was it yet light?"

Answer. "Just about dark."

Soldier, a Cherokee, was now called. On Soldier being introduced, Thomas Taylor, one of the jurors, observed, "Perhaps it is not my place to speak on such a subject; but if there is no impropriety, it might save the time of the Court should I remark that witness lives in my neighborhood, and has always had the character of a person so feeble in his capacity, that I should scarcely think him worth listening to on such an occasion. I have no knowledge of him, however, myself. I have only observed that he never talked much, nor seemed to pay much attention to any thing, or any body around him."

A rambling, conversational discussion followed,

which ended in a decision by the Judge, that the witness should be examined, and not interrupted, unless, from the manner in which he gave his evidence, it was obvious to the jury that he was incapable of observing or of reporting accurately.

Soldier, therefore, (who is a diminutive soft-spoken little Indian) being duly sworn, began:

"Myself and some others came to Peter's one evening, late—about dark. Peter asked me to play cards with him, which I did, until late."

Stand Watie, the counsel for the accused, here observed, "This has nothing to do with the affair before us. How can Peter's playing cards with Soldier, bear upon the case?"

The counsel for the nation replied, "I submit that the witness ought to begin at what point he likes. We shall soon see whether he comes to what may be important."

The accused had now risen from his place, and advanced close behind the bench of the witness, where he stood listening with apparently intense interest, for some time.

Meanwhile, the Judge exclaimed, "Let the witness proceed."

"Next morning we commenced playing again. Archilla Smith came to Peter's about twelve o'clock on that day. In the evening, we went to the Creek Camp, and there we found Archilla Smith, and Mac-

Intosh was also there; and pretty soon, he said, he would go to his sister's, but returned without going there; and pretty soon he came back to the Creek Camp. He then began to gallop his horse about, and would run his horse against Archilla Smith's horse, and make him break loose from the Creek man who held him. MacIntosh would also knock the boards off the camp. Sometime afterwards, Archilla Smith got mad, and went out, unbuttoning his coat at the same time. Archilla Smith and MacIntosh then commenced fighting. Archilla Smith had a knife and MacIntosh had a switch. I was myself still in the camp. Myself and some others then went out where they were fighting; and, when we got there, Archilla Smith put up his knife. MacIntosh then went off toward Peter's. He was well able to talk. As he went, he called Peter twice, and then ceased. I then proposed to go, and then we started. Archilla Smith followed us, and said he wanted us to go with him; but said he wanted to go to Peter's and get some whiskey first.

"After we left Peter's, Archilla Smith overtook us and said, 'this time, lest any person should waylay him, he would take his gun.' I then said to my companion, 'Perhaps he will do something to us.' We were afraid and tried to get out of his way."

The cross-examination of Soldier, was as follows:
"Did MacIntosh commence the affray?"

Answer. "No. Archilla Smith wanted to kill him."

Question. "How far from the fire was it that Archilla Smith and MacIntosh were fighting?"

Answer. "Very near."

Question. "Was the sun up yet?"

Answer. "No. It was almost dark."

Question. "Had you been drinking?"

Answer. "Not much."

Question. "Did you see Archilla Smith and MacIntosh fighting?"

Answer. "Yes."

Question. "How often did Archilla Smith stab MacIntosh?"

Answer. "Twice."

Question. "Did MacIntosh gallop off then?

Answer. "Yes. But he did not go far."

Question. "Did you go where MacIntosh was and examine him?"

Answer. "No. But he was stabbed. Archilla Smith kept urging us along."

Question. "Did you suppose he was asleep or dead?"

Answer. "I could not tell."

The counsel for the nation now observed, that no further testimony would be produced for the prosecution; and that the agents for the accused might bring forward their evidence.

John Young was called on by the agents for the accused, and sworn:

"I know nothing about what took place. Archilla Smith came to my house sometime *after dark;* and stayed until after breakfast at my house next morning. The day he left my house, in the evening, I heard that MacIntosh was dead. I saw nothing about Archilla Smith, or in his conversation, which led me to suspect that he had done anything."

The agents for the accused here desired that Eagle, a Cherokee, who was present, might be sworn on the part of the accused.

Counsel for the Nation—"For what purpose is Eagle introduced?"

Stand Watie. "To invalidate the testimony of those Creeks."

Counsel for the Nation. "Was he present when MacIntosh was killed?"

Stand Watie. "No; but he can give testimony with regard to several of the witnesses."

Counsel for the Nation. "I object to such testimony. It is entirely informal."

Stand Watie. "I appeal to the Judge, whether the testimony of Eagle ought not to be admitted."

Judge Price. "If you suppose that Eagle can give

testimony which may be important to the accused, let him give it."

Counsel for the Nation. "Does Eagle know the nature of an oath?"

Some conversation followed on that head, and the explanation of Eagle appearing satisfactory, the oath was administered.

"Do you know those Creeks who gave in their testimony while up?"

Answer. "Yes. I had them there working for me."

Question. "Have you had frequent conversation with them?"

Answer. "Yes; but I did not understand them.

Question. "Have you conversed with them about MacIntosh's death?"

Answer. "Yes."

Question. "Do you suppose they knew the nature of an oath?"

Answer. "I cannot tell."

The counsel for the nation here remarked, "They are judicious; and they know well enough that it is Indian against Indian, where truth must be spoken. The form of an oath may be new to them, without weakening their sense of the solemnity of the obligation to utter only what they know to be true. Our law entitles any one who will take an oath, to be heard. If the oath is violated, a punishment is provided."

Stand Watie, now turning to Eagle, asked, "Was not one of these witnesses once whipped for stealing?"

The counsel for the nation here interposed, and objected, and observed, "I object to the question, unless it can be shown, that the witness was whipped, if whipped at all, agreeable to law, and after a fair and impartial trial under the constitution and laws which have secured us against the possibility of being hurt unjustly."

Eagle, in the meantime, did not offer to make any answer. Stand Watie now asked Eagle, "Is it your opinion that the witness called Soldier is an idiot?"

The counsel for the nation replied, "The opinion of one witness concerning another, has nothing to do with the case. Soldier, or any other witness, must be judged by what he says; and that, not by any other witness, but by the jury. Idiot, or no idiot, Soldier has told a very straight story; a straighter story than some who are praised for good sense."

Here some one remarked, "It is easy enough to tell a straight story, when there is no one to make it crooked."

The counsel for the nation, then turning to Eagle, asked, "Do you know anything about the killing of John MacIntosh?"

Eagle answered, "I do not."

The counsel for the nation now asked, "Have the agents for the accused any more witnesses to produce?"

Stand Watie replied, "None."

Counsel for the Nation. "Nor have I."

Judge Price. "If the agents for the accused have any thing to say, or if the accused has any wish to speak, there is now an opening for either, or for all."

III

The Murder of John MacIntosh
Described

Stand Watie. "I am myself content to let the case go to the jury without comment. In my opinion, the testimony alone is quite sufficient to enable them to give a fair decision."

William Holt, *the associate agent with* Stand Watie *for the accused.*—"The evidence and the law are both before the jury. I see no use in wearying them with harangues. The case is so plain a one that it can speak for itself without further aid."

Upon this Isaac Busheyhead, the counsel for the nation, arose and addressed the Court, in Cherokee, as follows:

"Judge and Jurors,

By the Cherokee Nation, the prosecutor in the present case, I have been called upon to appear against one of our citizens for having taken the life of another. Deeply important as is the charge, and diffident as I feel of my own abilities to manage it as I could wish, I would fain have seen it placed in other hands; but denied as I am that indulgence, whatever my feeble powers may enable me to accomplish in furtherance of the mighty interests of public justice, shall be attempted fearlessly, earnestly and honestly. Stand

(34)

Watie, the agent for the accused, proposes to waive all remarks and that the evidence shall go at once before the jury for their decision. So does his other agent. I disagree with my friends upon this head. I consider that the life of an innocent man is of too much consequence to the community, to permit that it should be even endangered without strenuous efforts to elicit the truth or the untruth of the evidence against or for him by every possible variety of examination. If my opponent's friend is not guilty, it is as much due to him that he should have such an advantage for the proof that he is not so, as it is to the honor of the common country that an innocent citizen's blood should not call from the ground for retribution on his murderer, unheard. Since the adoption of our constitution and laws,[23] the blessings of protection to life and property

---

[23]The constitution of the Cherokee Nation was adopted at Tahlequah September 6, 1839, with a preamble reciting: "The Eastern and Western Cherokees having again reunited, and become one body politic, under the style and title of the Cherokee Nation; Therefore, We, the people of the Cherokee Nation, in National Convention assembled, in order to establish justice, insure tranquility, promote the common welfare, and to secure to ourselves and our posterity the blessings of freedom—acknowledging with humility and gratitude the goodness of the Sovereign Ruler of the Universe in permitting us so to do, and imploring His aid and guidance in its accomplishment —do ordain and establish this Constitution for the government of the Cherokee Nation."

It provided for three departments of government, legislative, executive and judicial. The legislative power of the government was "vested in two distinct branches, a National Committee and a Council." It directed the national council to lay off the Cherokee Nation

are beginning to be diffused far and wide. By the power
of this little volume (*producing the book of laws*) which
I hold in my hand, it has become our happiness, Judge
and Jurors, to check the wild career of roguery and
of bloodshed, and to enable our fellow countrymen to
place their heads upon their pillows, without apprehen-
sion either for their property or lives. Is there one of
you who does not look upon a volume fraught with
such magic, with gratitude and veneration?—Not one.—
The same volume which prescribes the law, and defines
the penalty for its violation, also secures to the injured
as well as to the accused, the privilege, and enjoins the
propriety, of thorough investigation before deciding
upon evidence. Is a debtor brought into court?—What
discussions do we hear either to vindicate or to discredit
the testimony on either side.—Is a thief arraigned?—
How strong would be the censures upon counsel that
would omit an effort to screen his client's property from
wrongful seizure, in the one case; or his person from
lashes and his character from infamy in the other,—

into eight districts. The national committee was to be composed of
two members from each district and the council of three from each
district, all to be elected every two years by the qualified electors
of the respective districts. The executive power of the nation was
vested in a principal chief, an assistant principal chief, and a treas-
urer. The judicial power was vested in a supreme court and such
inferior courts as the national council should provide. Provisions
for amending the constitution were made. A body of laws was
thereafter enacted by the national council pursuant to the constitution.

by sifting every particular alleged against him and in every shape!

"Here is a charge before us of a theft of a most awful description—a Cherokee's life stolen from him! —Here is a charge before us of a debt the most tremendous—the great debt of blood—a debt which the Creator tells us must be paid and never can be evaded; —and shall we treat this less seriously than we treat the commonest and the smallest of our transactions, by suffering its evidence to be slurred over without even a passing comment!—Surely not.

"I grant it is amiable enough in my opponent to desire that no stress should be placed upon the proof against his friend. He sees distinctly that Archilla Smith's guilt has been fully established by those proofs, and he is not willing to withhold from him the last desperate chance of escaping through the possible momentary and accidental inattention of some one of the jury, who may have chanced not to dwell so strongly on every part of the case as he himself had done. But generous as is his devotedness, it can avail nothing to the accused, in the face of his failure to weaken the overwhelming facts against him, even by the witnesses he has himself produced for his vindication and who could not utter one syllable in his favor!

"Judge and Jurors, though I have declined to acquiesce in my opponents' desire that I would be entirely silent, so irresistibly distinct is the evidence in the present case, that I need not trouble you at any length. You have the law before you, pronouncing that any person committing wilful murder shall be hanged by the neck until dead and that the execution shall take place within five days of the conviction, unless prevented by a respite or a pardon from the Principal Chief, accorded upon a petition from the neighbors of the offender, sanctioned by the judge and jury who have tried him. You have the warrant before you accusing Archilla Smith, the man who sits there, (*pointing to him*) with such a crime, committed upon the person of John MacIntosh. You have the evidence of no less than four witnesses, that they saw Archilla Smith stab MacIntosh once or twice; that they also saw him, after receiving these stabs, ride some hundred yards from the Creek camp, and then fell from his horse; that afterwards, they saw him, dead, his body gashed with a Bowie knife; and we have also shown that on the day following he was dressed, coffined and buried.— No attempt is made to deny, that the witnesses were perfectly well acquainted with the persons both of Archilla Smith and John MacIntosh; and no testimony is adduced to create even a doubt upon the facts sworn to and distinctly stated by the various witnesses.

"Judge and Jurors! If the great object of law is protection and redress, we are bound to claim it for every citizen equally. Laws are the wise substitutes provided in place of self protection. The accused is en-

titled to their guardianship in preventing an unfair
trial;—the dead is entitled to their redress for having
been forced before his time out of the world; and society
is entitled to their interposition to rid it of further danger from the murderer. Archilla Smith has incurred
a debt under your law, which can only be satisfied with
his blood. I shall say no more."

Stand Watie, the agent for the accused, immediately arose, and spoke (also in Cherokee) as follows:[24]

"Judge and Jurors,—I do not profess to be an
orator; I do not pretend to the power of answering
those who make a trade of public speaking, and whose
only aim is to reach their object by the shortest cuts,
without being at all reluctant to help themselves by taking every advantage upon the way. If such is the character of lawyers, I do not claim to be of their class: I
appear here only as a friend; and in rising to answer
a speech which seems to me entirely uncalled for, I rise
only because I consider that a friend in need is a friend
indeed; and that it would be injustice to the accused,

---

[24]While Stand Watie modestly deprecated his own talents he
demonstrated in later years that he was a man of intelligence and
resources. This was sufficiently indicated in his controversies
with the astute and learned John Ross during the succeeding years
and his leadership of a regiment of Confederate soldiers in the Civil
War. He was able to indict well composed letters and documents
of importance, many of which are to be seen in the *Phillips Collection* at the University of Oklahoma. Some of these letters with
an introduction and footnotes by Dr. E. E. Dale were published in
Chronicles of Oklahoma, I, 30.

to permit him to be assailed as he has been, without
showing that there are those who feel that such asser-
tions as are produced to crush him, however ground-
less, ought not to pass uncontradicted.

"The counsel against the accused, says he considers
his guilt as established. Of course, it is his business to
say so, however differently he may think. But, notwithstanding what he says, knowing him, as I do, to be
a man of sense, I believe he must, in reality think, as
every reflecting person cannot fail to think; and regard
the evidence adduced as entirely insufficient to sustain
the charge.

"That MacIntosh was killed I do not deny,. That
the witnesses saw him, I do not deny. But mark the
discrepancies in their narratives of what they saw!
One beheld the brawl, but says it was in daylight; another also beheld it, but says it was in the dark;—several persons were about and drinking at the time. If,
as sworn, the blow was given in the dark, and among
numbers,—and only heard, not seen,—can anyone safely pronounce by whom the blow was given?—all that
is distinctly proven amounts to this. There was a brawl;
and at some distance from where the brawl took place,
MacIntosh was afterwards found dead.

"Judge and Jurors! I trust you will bear in mind
the circumstances of the time when this sad event occurred. It occurred when a great deal of killing was
going on in this nation. That Archilla Smith had

some words with MacIntosh is possible enough; but
it is my firm belief that Archilla Smith—these idle
words being ended,—went off,—and that MacIntosh
quarreled with some new comer, who stabbed him in the
dark, and escaped.

"Judge and Jurors! You are all men and citizens
of truth and honor. You will weigh the well founded
doubts I have placed before you, because you must see
how strongly they are sustained by the contradictions
in the evidence,—and,—above all,—by those points of
the evidence which are the best entitled to belief. Consider how you would feel, should you discover when it
is too late, that what I have stated to you as most probable, is the fact, and that you have condemned the innocent. Imploring you to avoid that pang, I feel that
I may leave all the rest to independent minds like yours,
without fearing but that your verdict will be just,
and that it will restore the prisoner, who is accused so
wrongfully, to his home—his wife—his children;—and
to the native country which he loves, and may yet adorn
by a future career of usefulness and peace."

Here there was entire silence for awhile and no one
moved, until the counsel for the nation got up and remarked:

"If the other agent for the accused has any desire
to address the judge and jurors in his defense;—if any
other friend of his is present and has a wish to speak;—
there is now an opening and he can be heard: and if

the accused himself has aught to communicate, he also will be attentively listened to."

Another pause ensued, and, at length, the accused himself arose and spoke as follows:

"Presently after I asked the Judge whether I had the privilege to speak, the questions, which I had intended for the witnesses against me, were put to them by my friends. I did not, therefore, avail myself of the permission to speak; nor should I have done so now, but for some portion of the evidence subsequently given and which is of a nature entirely unexpected by me.— I allude to the declaration that I was seen to stab MacIntosh with a knife. An assertion of that sort could not but surprise me, considering that I was at the Creek camp, so very short a time; and, during the brief time, saw nothing whatever like killing. Thence I went to John Young's. It was only a little after dark that I went and I stayed there until some time after breakfast next morning, when I started for Peter's house, which is about two hundred yards from the place mentioned as the scene of the brawl; and then it was, for the first time, that I heard MacIntosh had fallen and saw him dead. After remaining a little while I went away with Peter Miller. Well: from that hour, to this trial, I never heard that MacIntosh was supposed to have been killed by me. This is the reason why I said that some portion of the evidence last given, took me by surprise. You have had John Young before you, of whom I spoke. He has told you I was there all night and till after breakfast, as I stated. He has specified, also, at what time I went away; and Young has declared to you, besides, that he never heard of MacIntosh's death until late on the next day's evening. I sent for Eagle to come and give his evidence in my favor. I meant to prove by Eagle that the Creeks who testified against me had told falsehoods. But, when Eagle came, he was only sworn to tell what he knew of the death of MacIntosh, and, as he said he knew nothing on that subject, he was not permitted to proceed, and the strong objections made by the counsel for the nation, shut out the proof I expected to obtain from him, that the Creeks had told falsehoods. I hope what has been done in this matter is borne out by the law; so you must arrange it in your own way, for I shall not trouble you again upon the affair."

As soon as the accused had resumed his place, the counsel for the Nation got up and addressed the court:

"I left my subject by observing that I could say no more; but so different is the appeal of my friend Stand Watie from anything I could have expected, that I feel it due to the country as well as to myself, to rise again, though only for a moment, and merely to express my disappointment at what I have heard. The agent for the accused led me to expect a reply to my address; a refutation of the distinct evidence I have produced. But, instead of a reply, he merely offers a conjecture; and calls upon you to believe only as much of the testimony as he is willing to infer; and to reject the rest. Is this a reply? Is this an argument? Ingenuous as may be the supposition of my friend Stand Watie,—after all, it is only a supposition;—and, as such we have no right to admit it in a solemn court of justice; especially, in the face of proven facts. I have only to desire that this may be borne in mind; and I now call upon you, Judge, to read the law, and to recapitulate the testimony, and to charge the Jury to decide the case."

The names of the Jurors were now called over and they, one by one, answered to them. The Judge, who called the roll, standing, retained the same position while he delivered the following charge, the Jurors also standing.

"Jurors, the law under which Archilla Smith, the prisoner now before you, has been arraigned, is to be found in our printed code, page seventeen, from which I will now read it at large.

'*An act for the punishment of criminal offenses.—Be it Enacted by the National Council, That, in all cases of wilful murder, the offender, upon trial and conviction by the authorized courts of this nation, shall suffer death by hanging; and, when sentence of death shall have been passed, the court shall grant a respite of five days before such criminal may be executed; but if the court, with the citizens generally of that section, shall deem it proper, they may petition the Principal Chief to pardon such convicted criminal, who may, if the reasons as set forth at large seem to warrant, grant an additional respite for a given number of days until he can assemble the assistant chief and Executive Council, who shall duly consider said petitions, with the circumstances and evidence given on trial, and decide by ordering his release and acquittal or execution.'*

"You have heard the evidence, Jurors, which has been produced to prove whether Archilla Smith has rendered himself liable to the penalty of this law. You have had so fair an opportunity of thoroughly studying this evidence, in the course of its first delivery, and its subsequent slow and careful translation into English, in your presence,—that I should only waste your time and tire your patience by any attempt at recapitulation. You can take the minutes of the testimony, as recorded, out with you, and you can weigh them.

"I trust none of you have any prejudice against the accused, and that you will all of you bear in mind that you break your solemn oath if you permit yourselves to consider anything in forming your judgment, but these facts which you conscientiously believe to have been unquestionably proven. There appears to me much in the evidence that bears heavily against Archilla Smith; and much too, of a suspicious complexion. I would beg you most scrupulously to separate the doubtful from the less doubtful; and not to permit any thing unsure to operate upon your verdict. It is a maxim, in these cases, of all good men, that it is better for ten guilty to escape than for one who is innocent to suffer. Bear this in mind, and if you feel in the slightest degree as if the accused has been accused wrongfully, let him be acquitted. We meet here only to do impartial justice to the living as well as to the dead; and he who is arraigned, and he who has gone to his account, are equally entitled to it at your hands, and, I am persuaded, will receive it equally."

The jurors now left the cabin and withdrew to a place where a large fire had been lighted in the open air upon a distant rising ground; and all persons were prevented from approaching them.

The Judge was left in the court room, before the fire. The accused remained sitting on the bench he had occupied from the first, and by his side an Indian compatriot guarding him with a loaded gun. There was no one else in the cabin excepting myself. Deep silence prevailed. On a sudden, tears gushed down the cheeks of the Judge. He covered his face with both hands. I stood by his side and he exclaimed,

"Lend me your pocket handkerchief," and wept and sobbed like a child. The accused did not utter a word, but his eager eyes were strained upon the Judge, with an expression utterly indescribable.

The jury could not come to any conclusion that night. On the 18th day of December, 1840,

The Fourth Day of Trial

it appeared that two of them could not be brought to agree with the rest. In the afternoon of that day, they came into court, and affirmed that they never would be able to make up a verdict and prayed to be discharged from further consideration of the case. After some demur, the Judge consented to their discharge, adjourned the court until Tuesday, the 22d of December, 1840.

On the evening of the first jury's decision, the three young sons of Archilla Smith were among the numerous guests at the abode of the Principal Chief.[25] They, like the other visitors, according to the custom of the country, walked in and took their meals and rest like familiar friends.[26] They were recognized and treated

---

[25] John Ross then lived in a double story-and-a-half log house at Park Hill.

[26] In another account Payne described the custom of countless numbers of people who stopped at the home of Chief Ross to be fed: "At meals, as many as the table can accommodate, sit down indiscriminately; and outside the door which stands always wide open, two or three dogs are intently eyeing the table from the threshhold, and Indians in their blankets, as earnestly watching it in silence, and waiting their turn to be invited in. Thus, set after set is summoned, till all are satisfied. The housekeeper never knows here whether she has to lodge and feed twenty-five or fifty or double the number. But the guests seldom fall far below the five and twenty. This uncertainty often creates a puzzle for supplies; and apologies are often made for scanty fare or an omitted meal; sometimes, for weeks together, the dinner and supper are blended; and one day's hours for either afford no guide for another's; they come as it happens." This open and indiscriminate hospitality made a severe levy on the resources of Chief Ross, but it was a custom in the tribe that no one thought of avoiding. Any passing Cherokee was

affectionately. One of them went out to play with the
Principal Chief's youngest son.—"Who is your mother?" was asked of one. "Ate," he replied—which is
the name of Archilla Smith's last wife. Each of
the three sons, it is said, was by a different mother.
Ate was reported on the same evening to have taken
up her lodging at the habitation of the Principal Chief's
brother, Lewis Ross,²⁷ in the immediate neighborhood.
Her own dwelling was at some distance and she and the
family wished to be near the accused, who was under
guard only a short way from the residences of the
Rosses.

---

welcomed almost as a matter of right to share the food with any
other as long as it lasted. And any possible host who would deny
that boon to another was as much disgraced as the traveler would
be who declined the offer. This custom had its objections as it en-
couraged idleness and improvidence. "Sauntering from one house to
another, eating his neighbor out of house and home" as expressed
by one observing Cherokee (*The Arkansas Advocate* (Little Rock),
February 15, 1832).

²⁷John Ross lived on the north side of the creek at Park Hill
and his brother Lewis on the south side a quarter of a mile distant.
When Hitchcock was there the next year he described the surround-
ings: "Lewis Ross the merchant is wealthy and lives in considerable
style. His house is of the cottage character, clapboarded and painted;
his floor carpeted, his furniture elegant, cane bottomed chairs, of
high finish, mahogany sofa, two superior mahogany Boston rocking
chairs, mahogany ladies work table with drawers, a very superior
Chickering piano on which his unmarried daughter, a young lady of
about 17 or 18, just from school in Rawway in New Jersey, plays
some waltzes, and sings some songs. She is lively and pretty with
rich flowing curls, very fine eyes and beautiful regular ivory teeth"
(Hitchcock, *op. cit.*, 45). The Lewis Ross house is still standing.

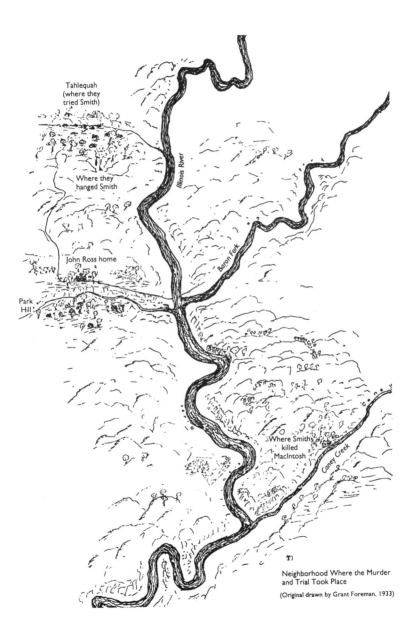

Tahlequah
(where they
tried Smith)

Where they
hanged Smith

John Ross home

Park
Hill

Illinois River

Baron Fork

Where Smith
killed
MacIntosh

Caney Creek

Neighborhood Where the Murder
and Trial Took Place

(Original drawn by Grant Foreman, 1933)

STAND WATIE

JOHN ROSS
Photograph of oil portrait in possession of Oklahoma Historical Society.

JESSE BUSHYHEAD

IV

STAND WATIE OPPOSES A SECOND TRIAL;
JUDGE BUSHYHEAD EXPOUNDS THE LAW

Washington City, March 11, 1841.

Presently after the proceedings detailed in my letter of yesterday, on December 18, 1840, Judge Price proved to be extremely ill. The Cherokee law requires that the list of persons to compose a jury, shall be supplied by the Judge; and, in obedience to the law, the counsel for the nation and for the accused, called upon Judge Price to name twenty-four good men in the district, that a jury might be selected from the list. But the illness of Judge Price, rendering it impossible for him to attend to business, the counsellors on both sides met, and, I understand, it was agreed to leave it to the counsel for the accused to form a list, which being done, and submitted to the judge, he approved.

The illness of Judge Price continuing, he sent to the Principal Chief, requesting to be permitted to resign his seat. At the same time, the High Sheriff gave information that, owing to the illness of Judge Price, public business was obstructed and execution of the laws delayed. The Principal Chief, under the 10th Section, in the 4th article of the Cherokee Constitution, which says, *"He shall take care that the laws be faithfully executed"* forthwith instructed the High Sheriff to see that all unfinished business should be taken up, and with-

out delay completed according to the constitution and
the laws. The High Sheriff immediately called upon
the Chief Justice of the Supreme Court to attend the
special court and to preside over it in place of Judge
Price, the district judge, for the unfinished trial of
Archilla Smith. Accordingly, Jesse Bushyhead,[28] Chief

[28]The Rev. Jesse Bushyhead was a Baptist minister and an ex-
ceptionally useful man to his tribe. He conducted one of the emigrating parties of Cherokee of whom he delivered 898 in their new
home February 23, 1839. He not only preached to his people in
Cherokee but he interpreted for other preachers who spoke only in
English. Hitchcock saw him "a good looking rather portly man, 35
or 40 years of age. . . He is very fluent and easy (as a speaker)
not affectedly an actor. He is truly an interesting man. . . Considered,the best interpreter in the Nation. He is universally respected
and beloved. His mere opinion in the Nation has great weight and
his persuasion upon almost any subject can win the people to his
views. He is a fair minded man and if he can be satisfied, the Nation ought to acquiesce. If he is not satisfied it may suggest a
doubt whether some concessions may not be proper. The united
opinion of Bushyhead and Benge will be entitled to great consideration, for it will be decisive with the nation, even against John Ross,
though the latter of the two will be slow in differing from him"
(Hitchcock op. cit., 37, 38, 47, 52, 233, 234). After the removal,
Bushyhead conducted the Baptist mission north of the site of the
present Westville, Oklahoma, where he died July 17, 1844. He was
buried near the mission. "His disinterestedness in the feudal and
political troubles among his people gained for him the peculiar distinction of being the only man of any consequence among the Cherokees who habitually traveled among his people in the troublous
period of 1839-46 unarmed, except, as he said with his Bible" (Em-
met Star, History of the Cherokee Indians, 256). " 'Jesse Bushyhead,
Chief Justice of the Supreme Court of the Cherokees . . . was a
person of great distinction among his tribe. He was in his acquire-
ments a self-made man. He obtained in his youth, a very limited
English education, which he improved to enable him to be a good
English speaker, as well as an able orator in the Cherokee. He was

Justice of the Cherokee Supreme Court took his seat, on the 22d of December, 1840, being

THE FIFTH DAY OF TRIAL:

when, the court being duly organized, the following list of persons summoned as jurors was produced.

Young Wolf	John Looney
Richard Ratcliff	JESSE WOLF
Sul-la-te-sky Watts	Lewis Melton
George Chambers	Jesse Russell
Little Chicken	Pheasant
Ta-la-se-my	Jack Nicholson

a correct interpreter and translator, and at his demise was extensively engaged in translating English into Cherokee. He has occupied many public stations, which he discharged with fidelity and for the good of his people. His name will live as long as his tribe, while his exulting spirit has joined the righteous in heaven'."

"The above merited tribute is paid by *The National Intelligencer* (Washington, D. C.) to our late beloved fellow-citizen and Chief Justice, the Rev. Jesse Bushyhead. Besides the arduous and responsible duties which devolved upon him as Chief Justice of the Supreme Court of the Cherokee Nation, duties which he ever discharged with fidelity, ability, and impartiality, Mr. B. was at the time of his death, actively engaged in preaching the gospel to his countrymen, and translating the sacred Scriptures into his native language. He was also President of the Cherokee Bible and Temperance Society.

"He was a man of good natural sense, upright in his dealings, exemplary in his conduct, kind in feeling, independent in character, and one who had deeply at heart the welfare of his whole people, among whom he strove to inculcate the principles of order, industry, and religion. His death, in the prime of life and usefulness, has caused a loss to his bereaved family and the country at large, which none can supply" (*Cherokee Advocate,* September 26, 1844, p. 3, col. 4).

James Pritchet

WILLIAM GRIMMET

Killemore

Pigeon

James Starr Jun.

Stephen Hildebrand

James Lowery

Arch. Campbell

Jackson R. Gourd

Benjamin Vann

Daniel Nave*

Jack Spears*

The first names on the foregoing list were adopted
by the accused, and consequently those following them
were omitted. One name, which is printed in small
capitals, was objected to by the counsel for the prosecution, as not residing within the district. Another did
not wish to serve, and after some discussion, was discharged. For these the two names at the end of the
list, with stars affixed to them, were added, to make up
the twenty-four from whom a choice was to be made.
The names standing above in Roman letters at length
constituted the Jury. Young Wolf,[29] who was made

---

[29]Young Wolfe was a Cherokee preacher who lived on the east
side of the creek on the hill overlooking the council ground at Tahlequah. When Hitchcock came there he stopped at Young Wolfe's
house: "And what do I find—one of the neatest and most comfortable log houses I almost ever saw. Mr. Wolfe is a half-breed, a
very portly large man (has a large arm chair expressly made for
him) speaks very good English, positively better than many of our
country farmers in the West and South. His wife (strange) is a
Dutch woman. I suppose she speaks English, but I have not heard
her open her lips. Two young women, both speaking very good
English have been sewing in the room since they gave me dinner,
pork ribs, sliced and fried sweet potatoes, good biscuit of fresh
flour (wheat) and a cup of tea, sugar and milk, all on a clean table
cloth. . . . I retired early last evening leaving 6 to 8 Cherokees in

foreman, is a native preacher, of the Methodist persuasion.

The jury being sworn, the counsel for the nation,
Isaac Bushyhead, read the warrant against the accused,
as before, and then observed (in Cherokee) :

"Such, Judge and Jurors, is the case before you.
Ample testimony has been already given to prove that
Archilla Smith is guilty of this charge, and the testimony in question was carefully translated upon the
spot into English,—thoroughly canvassed and examined, during the progress of the translation, and, in this
place, openly written down;—and I now place it before
the court, to be submitted for your consideration."

William Holt, one of the counsel, or agents, for
the accused, now arose:

"I object to any further proceeding in this case.
I object to a second jury and a second judge. It is
expressly provided in section 6 of article 6, in the Constitution adopted at Tahlequah, and you will find it
inscribed in page 14 of the printed copy: *No person*

---

quiet conversation in the Cherokee language. About half past 9 (I
heard the clocks, for there are two in the house strike 10 soon
after the service) I was awakened by the singing of a hymn, after
which I heard the prayer. This morning I was present at the service, a clergyman read a psalm or hymn sung, prayer all in Cherokee, all conducted in perfect propriety and the prayer was uttered
from the heart" (Hitchcock 37). Rev. Young Wolfe was born November 20, 1792, and died June 29, 1843, and the marble monument
marking his grave stands on the hill overlooking the town of Tahlequah.

shall for the same offense be twice put in jeopardy of life or limb.

"I claim for Archilla Smith the benefit of this law, which protects every citizen from being twice tried for the same offense."

The Counsel for the nation, in reply, observed:

"I would submit to the court that I consider the objection made by my friend opposite, as one which cannot for a moment be entertained. This is not a second trial;—it is only a continuation of the first;—a continuation assented to by both parties, and under circumstances and on conditions in which both have equally acquiesced. The difficulty arising from the failure of the first jury to decide, has been promptly met by the Principal Chief, who is compelled by the constitution to prevent any interruption in the due course of the law. *'He shall take care'* says the tenth section of article the fourth in that constitution, as you will find in page the 9th of the printed copy, *'He shall take care that the laws be faithfully executed.'* Finding this trial yet undecided, the Executive called upon the Sheriff to look to it, and the Sheriff summoned a new jury. The sudden and severe illness of the Judge who has thus far presided, rendering his further attendance impossible, he resigned; and the duty thus devolving upon another, our Chief Justice has obeyed the summons to bring this unfinished matter to a close. From the time when the accused was arrested, up to the present moment, I consider the case in progress; and so it will continue, until a jury brings in a verdict. I therefore submit that the case ought to proceed without further delay."

No reply being made by the opposite counsel, the Chief Justice directed the list of jurors to be again produced and called over. All answered to their names. The counsel for the nation handed the written report of the testimony to the Chief Justice. The Chief Justice desired the Foreman of the jury to interpret the English translation in Cherokee, for that part of the jury who did not understand English. The Foreman observed that he did not consider himself sufficiently acquainted with English to translate the testimony so fully and faithfully as was requisite, and he must therefore decline. He would prefer that the Chief Justice himself should do it; the jury would be better satisfied and the interpretation would be better made.

The Chief Justice then read the entire testimony as reported already in my former letters, translating it to the jury back into Cherokee.

The counsel for the nation then arose and said:

"Judge and Jurors:—The arrangements for bringing the case now before us, to a close, being at length satisfactorily completed, it becomes again my duty to explain the accusation, which I will do as briefly as I can consistently with my desire to put the new jury in full possession of all the facts.

"The warrant against the accused sets forth that in the latter part of the fall, or early in the winter, of 1839, John MacIntosh was wilfully murdered on Caney by Archilla Smith. You are aware of the penalty for wilful murder. The same law which declares the punishment, enjoins that it shall not be inflicted without proofs, the most distinct and positive, of guilt. Such proofs have been produced and are now in your possession.

"Upon the part of the accused, no evidence has been offered, which can either invalidate the testimony against him, or establish aught in his favor to counteract it. To dwell further upon the subject, would, therefore, be only a wanton intrusion upon your time; and, therefore, unless something unexpected should arise to require my speaking again, I shall submit it to your uncompromising sense of duty and of justice, without further comment."

Stand Watie, the agent of the accused, replied as follows:

"Judge and Jurors, I know you all and know you well. I know you to be men who will do that which is right yourselves and prevent others, where you have influence, from doing otherwise than right. With you, therefore, I feel safe; and I feel, too, that my friend Archilla Smith is safe, because I am convinced that

he did not kill John MacIntosh. We do not deny that
MacIntosh was killed and killed at the time and place
asserted; but we do deny that anything is proven in the
evidence, further than that MacIntosh was killed.
One witness swears that he saw Archilla Smith *strike*
MacIntosh with a knife;—another saw him *stab* Mac-
Intosh with a knife *twice;* another that he saw him
stab MacIntosh with a knife *once.* There is the same
vagueness and variation in respect to the time when
the mischief occurred. One swears it was *in the day
light;* another that it was *in the dark;* and one thinks
Archilla Smith must have been the murderer, because
Archilla Smith and John MacIntosh had a few
words near the Creek camp, and, at a field not far from
thence he afterwards found John MacIntosh a corpse.
Is this evidence sufficient to justify the destruction of a
man's life and character; widowhood to his wife; or-
phanage to his children and infamy upon his name?

"But, for the sake of argument, suppose for a moment that John MacIntosh *did* fall by the hand of
Archilla Smith. What is there in the evidence, ad-
mitting it to the fullest extent, that can convict Archilla
Smith of wilful murder?

"It will be recollected that at the moment when
this sad event occurred, confusion prevailed throughout
our land. Assassinations were common. Three of the
particular friends of Archilla Smith had just then

fallen,[30] and had not fallen without some hand to strike
the blow; and of the only offense ever charged against
them as its cause, Archilla Smith had been a con-
spicuous sharer.   It has been proven by the evidence
that MacIntosh dashed whooping, and in a threatening
manner, against the Creek camp where Archilla
Smith was; and why may he not have fancied 'now
my turn is come,' and, in the phrenzy of the moment,
inflicted a blow unknowingly, or in self defense?   All

---

[30]The reference is to the brutal murder of Elias Boudinot,
Major Ridge and his son, John Ridge. They were the leaders among
the signers of the fraudulent treaty of 1835. Their action was be-
lieved by them to offer the only solution of the intolerable situation
in which the tribe was found in the East, but they were regarded
by thousands who opposed their views as traitors to the tribe and
the authors of the suffering they endured on their removal in 1839.
These recent arrivals numbered more than twice those who had
preceded them and there ensued an intense feeling of hostile rivalry
for control of the tribal government. A meeting was held at Taka-
tokah, or Double Springs, northwest of Tahlequah in June, 1839,
where an effort was made to unite the factions under a common
government. The Old Settlers and Treaty Party factions resisted
the formation of a new government dominated by the Ross faction
and the meeting broke up on the twentieth in complete failure. Before the Indians dispersed, the Ross people reconvened and called
another meeting for July 1 to meet southeast of Tahlequah. The
next day the country was thrown into great excitement by the murder of the three leaders of the Treaty Faction. Boudinot was engaged in building his house at Park Hill when he left to accompany
three men to the home of Doctor Worcester to secure some medi-
cine for them; about half way there his companions seized and killed
him, and cut him to pieces with knives and tomahawks. Major Ridge
was killed at Beatties Prairie near the Arkansas line, and his son
was taken from bed and cut to pieces with tomahawks at his home
in northeastern Indian Territory. Notwithstanding the frequent

the witnesses concur in depicting the scene as one of riot, drinking and confusion; but which of them offers the slightest intimation that Archilla Smith had exhibited signs of settled malice? If, therefore, my supposition for the sake of argument is for a moment admitted,—can even this bring Archilla Smith's life into jeopardy for wilful murder? Surely not. At most, it could have been no more than accident,—a mistaken movement for self-defense; or even if an act of manslaughter,—such an act, according to our laws, does not incur the extreme penalty for murder. To suppose for a moment that Archilla Smith deliberately desired to kill John MacIntosh appears to me absurd.

charges, there was never any evidence that John Ross had anything to do with the killings, but it was obvious that they were committed by some of the recent emigrants.

The meeting was held in July and in spite of the opposition of the earlier arrivals and of the military who took the part of the minority, an act of union was adopted and later a constitution, under which the Cherokee Nation flourished as long as it continued its tribal existence. Under the new regime Ross served many years as chief and his administration was at first marked by a stern and uncompromising attitude towards the minority, many of whom in turn resisted the successful operation of the new government. The result for five or six years was a state of disorder and a long list of homicides by both sides; the minority committed murders without warrant of law and the governing faction committed similar excesses, sometimes in the name of the law. Life and property were not safe and a state of almost civil war existed. Many of the minority faction took refuge in neighboring Arkansas and some of them under the leadership of Stand Watie fortified themselves at old Fort Wayne. A few left for Texas and more would have gone there but for the adjustment of difficulties achieved by the new treaty of 1846, which ended the reign of terror.

"But, Judge and Jurors, though I have imagined a case, which, while it will permit our believing all the evidence, will not, at the same time, bring the accused within the reach of that law under which he is arraigned, —I am convinced that Archilla Smith did not kill John MacIntosh, even by accident,—even for self-defense;—but that he is entirely innocent of killing him at all. I believe, too, that such will be your own impression, when you have carefully sifted the evidence, and weighed its sources. So well am I acquainted, gentlemen, with all of you; so thorough is my confidence in your moderation and your truth, that I cannot entertain a fear for my wronged friend. On the contrary, I trust, ere many hours, to see him restored to society,— and enjoying and reciprocating peace and friendship with all his fellow citizens, and even rejoicing in the temporary annoyance he has endured because it will prove that whatever misunderstandings may arise among us, magnanimity and truth must at last prevail."

The counsel for the nation thus answered:

"Judge and Jurors,—I did not suppose I should think it necessary to trouble you again upon so clear a case as the one now before us; but my friend Stand Watie has said things which I am at a loss to comprehend and will, no doubt, enlighten me if I name them.

"First, he denies that Archilla Smith killed John MacIntosh: Secondly, he appears to admit that Ar-

chilla Smith did kill John MacIntosh, but that he did
so in self defense: Thirdly, he again admits the killing by Archilla Smith, but ascribes it to accident.

"Surely, after the distinct proofs I have given of
this murder, all argument is superfluous, unless the evidence produced can be discredited,—which has not yet
been done. Four witnesses have sworn to the act. One,
saw Archilla Smith stab John MacIntosh once;
another, twice;—another saw Archilla Smith hit
John MacIntosh, or stab him, once or twice with a
knife; another saw the same. Four men were present
at the brawl,—three swear it was commenced by
Archilla Smith; four saw the bowie knife in Archilla Smith's hand, and, with that knife MacIntosh
was seen to be stabbed. The same witnesses a short
time subsequently beheld John MacIntosh dead a few
yards from the creek camp; saw the bowie-knife gash
upon his body, and attended the attiring of the corpse
for burial and its final consignment to the grave. These
four all knew him to be Oh-Kungh-Skee, or otherwise, John MacIntosh. They had known him before
he was killed; they knew him again after they saw him
dead. They also knew Archilla Smith. All four
of them have looked upon the accused as he sits yonder,
and have pronounced that he it was who did this murder. What further evidence of guilt can be required?

"As for the second point attempted by my friend

Stand Watie, that if Archilla Smith did kill John MacIntosh, it was done in self-defense, surely it is somewhat late to put forth a pretext like that. If such had been the excuse of the accused, would he have thus long omitted to wage it? Would he not, in the very outset of the case, have manfully come forward,—owned that he had been assailed and had conquered his assailant and not have thus deferred to speak, until after he saw himself proven guilty of the crime of murder.

"Precisely the same argument confutes the third apology invented by my opponent!—Accident forsooth! Where is the proof? Where is the remotest likelihood that this was done by accident?

"The case mentioned by Stand Watie of three particular friends of Archilla Smith, who had fallen before this murder,—and whose fall, he imagines, may have made Archilla Smith deem his own life in danger,—is not one upon which I desire to dwell; for it appears to me unnecessary on an occasion like this to advert to any difficulties which may have existed among our people; especially when, as I hope and trust is now the case, these difficulties have given way to universal peace and friendship and to the union of all parties for the common good I am at a loss to conceive how the fall of these three persons, some four or five months prior to the union among us, and to the oblivion of all dissentions, could have any bearing upon an act like the one now awaiting judgment. Surely my worthy friend could scarcely be aware of what he said, when he insinuated, that, because three particular friends of Archilla Smith had fallen, Archilla Smith had a right to kill some one in return. There is no community within my knowledge, that would not, at this age of the world, shudder at a doctrine which would thus expose the innocent.—Alas! Archilla Smith is not the man to refrain from harshness until compelled by danger or tempted by accident. From my earliest knowledge of him,—and this now dates back many years,—he has been notorious for his love of quarrel and of fight. No matter who the person, or what the provocation, his fist, his club, his knife, his pistol, his tomahawk, his rifle, never rested. Of this, scarcely a man within hearing of my voice but is aware. Sometimes, he will disable his antagonist with a shot or with a stone or club, or gash him with a knife; or, sometimes, be himself disabled and receive upon his person, the enduring evidence of his reckless life and character, which at this very moment may be read from head to foot there in deep scars.—Is it probable that such a man would be over-scrupulous about motives for a deed of blood; or only be capable of it for self-defense or through mere accident?

"The only real difficulty in the present case, appears to have arisen from some misconceptions with regard to

evidence, of which my friend Stand Watie has done
his best to avail himself—and that with much ingenuity.
I allude to objections on the score of a want of entire
conformity in minor points of evidence from different
sources; although in substance the conformity is complete.   The misconception it was, I am told, that produced the failure of the first jury to decide; and as it
is proper you should be fully informed upon the question it involves of fitting evidence, perhaps I cannot
make myself better understood than by explaining it
through an incident by no means rare among our people.

"Two men are transacting business, and one of them
desires to give the other a promissory note; but neither
of them knowing how to write, they obtain the aid of
an amanuensis.   The promissory note is prepared, and
in place of a signature the giver must affix his mark.   A
witness is called.   The giver of the note is desired to
touch the quill-top with his finger, while the amanuensis
forms a cross upon the paper.   The witness is then requested to take notice, that he may give his attestation.
Sometimes in the same glance, he sees the giver's finger
at the pen-top; and the mark affixed by the amanuensis
under it;—but, sometimes, observing neither the one nor
the other, he merely asks whether the writing in the paper is what it pretends to be, and being informed by all
parties that it is, on that acknowledgment he considers
himself authorized to make the attestation.   It has hap-

pened that a debt thus incurred has been denied;—that
the signing by the cross-mark has been denied;—or that
the signer, dying, the claim could only be collected from
his estate. If the witness, in either case, is called upon,
it matters not whether he has seen the pen-top touched,
or the mark inscribed, or only heard the act confessed;
—if he can swear to either, it renders the note as bind-
ing as if he should swear to all. Nay, even if three witnesses have been present, and one has only seen the pen-
top touched,—another only the cross-mark made,—and
a third only heard the mark confessed; the want of uni-
formity in their evidence does not discredit the note;—
each proves equally that it is valid, though each proves
it in a different way. Execution then issues, and the
officers of justice must collect the debt.

"Such is the position of the present charge against
Archilla Smith. All the witnesses concur in all the
essential particulars, though all may not have seen exact-
ly the same part of the entire act to which all bear testimony. The mighty debt has in this way been proven
against Archilla Smith, and now it only remains for
execution to issue, and for the officers of justice to claim
that by which human life taken wantonly can alone be
satisfied. John MacIntosh is as much entitled to the
protection of law as Archilla Smith; and if he has
been deprived by violence of the power to do himself
justice, it becomes the more imperative on us to do it

for him. We owe this much to all society that survives him. We cannot, indeed, bring him from the grave; but by a signal act of retribution upon his destroyer, we may shield our families from the assassin, and prevent future disturbance of our country by the unprincipled and the violent.—Then will the spirit of the murdered be appeased,—and nobly!

"Jurors! Some of you have sons as liable as was John MacIntosh to being cut off in the prime of life and hope—some of you are members of the church—all of you have held up your right hands, and have sworn before your Maker, God, that you will do justice between man and man.—Jurors! Do not forget your oath."

Chief-Justice Bushyhead now arose, and having called over the names of the jury, to which each answered,—he charged them, in Cherokee as follows:

"Before the introduction of written laws among our people, we had a custom which often made the innocent suffer for the guilty. Killing at that time occurred as frequently as it does now; but, at that time, when any individual belonging to one of our seven clans" was killed, the clan of which the slain was a

---

"The seven clans of the Cherokee were "Ani-wa ya (Wolf), Ani-Kawi (Deer), Ani-Tsi skwa (Bird), Ani-wa di (Paint), Ani-Saha ni, Ani-Ga tagwi, and Ani-Gi-la hi. The names of the last three can not be translated with certainty. There is evidence that there were anciently 14, which by extinction or absorption have been reduced to their present number (*Handbook of American Indians*, I, 247). No Cherokee could marry into the clan of his father or

member, had a right to exact a life from the clan of the slayer. There was no specific injunction with regard to the manner of execution, nor was there any rule prescribed even as to the person to be selected for death, in the event of difficulty in finding the slayer himself;— the nearest relative of the slain was to take the life of any one he chose in the slayer's clan; and thus it was that the innocent was often made to suffer for the guilty.

"Even after the introduction of written laws among our people, the ancient law of the clans still prevailed. It seems to have been prized among us more than any other. The constitution adopted in our old nation east of the Mississippi provided a substitute more equitable;—still, whenever a life was taken, the nearest relative of the slain considered himself solemnly bound to look to the slayer's clan for a life in return.

"I mention the written laws of the old nation" east

---

mother. "If the murderer fled his brother or nearest relative was liable to suffer in his place. If a man killed his brother he was amenable to no one. If the murderer (this however is known only by tradition) was not as respectable as the murdered—his relative, or a man of his clan of a more respectable standing was liable to suffer" (*Cherokee Phoenix,* February 18, 1829, p. 2, col. 5).

[32]A few laws were reduced to writing before 1827, but in that year a constitution was determined on. However, at that time their chief Path Killer died. The second chief, Charles R. Hicks, then became chief but he served only a week when he, too, died. Then, by operation of their laws, the president of the council, John Ross, became chief and served from January until October, when William Hicks, the son of Charles Hicks, was appointed chief, and John Ross second chief. Delegates from the districts were designated,

of the Mississippi, and the constitution adopted there, because laws and a constitution substantially the same, now govern us in the west. The ancient exactions of the clan are abolished and we have adopted a system more in accordance with our improved views of what is fair and right. When a man is slain now, his destruction is to be avenged, not only by his relations, but by his country. It instantly becomes imperative on the officers of the nation, especially the Sheriff, to arrest the slayer, and to bring him before a court for trial.— When there, his case must be carefully examined, and if the most unquestionable proofs appear that he is guilty, he must then suffer the extreme penalty of the law, but only in the event of proofs unquestionable; for it is the principle of our present written law, not to harm the innocent.

"The law under which the prisoner now before you is arraigned, I will read to you in full. (*The Chief Justice then read, in Cherokee, the law which I have quoted in a former letter.*)

"You will perceive that in this statute, there is no reference whatever to the ancient rules of the clan-kin, but that, without reference to clans, the accused can only be convicted in the event of its being plainly proven

---

coincident with the plans to start a newspaper. They met in July and adopted a constitution and John Ross was elected chief. The Western Cherokees had begun enacting and recording laws in 1820. They, for a time, had a first, second and third chief, but later the three chiefs were placed upon the same footing.

against him that his own hand did the murder. To this principle I would especially direct your attention. Some of you, possibly, may be of the same clan with the deceased. If so, remember that your oath binds you to forget your clan-kin; and only to be guided in your decision by the evidence of the prisoner's innocence or guilt.

"In carefully sifting this evidence and in concluding upon the case, I would farther enjoin upon you, Jurors, and that emphatically, to remember that the only point which you have a right to consider in this matter is the charge against Archilla Smith for murdering John MacIntosh. Whatever you may know or have heard about him or his actions or his character before, must be dismissed entirely from your minds. You break your oath if you allow any impression whatever to mingle with the proofs for or against this single charge. You break your oath equally if you permit the political difficulties under which the nation laboured not long since, and to which the counsel on both sides have made some allusion, in any way to influence your judgment. You have no right to believe evil of Archilla Smith, because you may object to his course in politics; —you have no right to shrink from condemning him, if guilty, from the fear that your condemnation may be ascribed to political prejudices. You must keep yourselves equally free from the desire to be vindictive or to show mercy;—the one would make you the criminal instead of him whom you would condemn;—the other is the prerogative of a department of our government, to which we have ourselves prescribed regulations for its exercise. Your duty bids you examine testimony; and to give your honest verdict fearlessly, whenever you are convinced; and may you be guided to such a judgment as your conscience may never hereafter disapprove."

V

THE SIXTH DAY: DELIBERATION OF THE JURY

The jury now withdrew. They took the written notes of the testimony with them and remained all night in close consultation; and on Wednesday, December 23, 1840, being

THE SIXTH DAY OF TRIAL

the jury came into court in the morning. The Foreman observed to the Chief Justice:

Foreman of the Jury.—"I am desired to state that the jury find it entirely impossible to come to any decision upon this case."

Chief Justice.—"The rights of the accused and of the nation equally require a decision; and a decision, one way or the other, must be given. If the accused is not guilty, it is unfair and injurious to detain him;—if guilty, it is equally hurtful to him and to all, to procrastinate a decision, which, sooner or later, must be made."

The jury withdrew and remained together all day. In the evening they came back into court. The Foreman remarked:

Foreman of the Jury.—"It is the wish of the Jury that they may have the privilege of seeing the witnesses face to face; and of asking a few questions in explanation of their evidence."

Chief Justice.—"The accused and the jury are entitled to that privilege. Sheriff, call the witnesses."

High Sheriff.—"They are not here. Some of them have returned to their homes, many miles distant."

Chief Justice.—"Let them be forthwith sent for and brought before the Jury."

The jury now retired and remained in consultation again all night. On the following morning, Thursday the 24th of December, 1840, being

THE SEVENTH DAY OF TRIAL

they sent for the Chief Justice, who forthwith attended them, when the Foreman of the Jury thus addressed him:

Foreman of the Jury.—"The Jury have sent for you, Judge, in order to receive from you some explanations in relation to what ought to be understood by the expression *'accidental killing;'* by the expression *'killing in self-defense;'* and by the expression *'wilful murder.'*

"The Jury also desire some information about the different sorts of evidence; and would be glad of your instructions as to what ought to be considered as *'circumstantial evidence'* and what ought to be considered as *'point blank evidence.'* "

It may not be irrelevant for me to mention here that the difficulty of discriminating in such cases as the one now under review, between the different shades of guilt incurred by different sorts of killing, is probably much greater to an Indian than a white man. The ancient Indian system, I believe, made it necessary to take life for life, whether the killing was by chance or malice; and even to this day, in many tribes, the death by accident must be avenged precisely in the same way as the death by design. Understanding this, your readers will be better able to appreciate the necessity for the questions of the Cherokee Jury, and the force of the following reply made to them by the Chief Justice.

Chief Justice.—"I will comply with your desire to the best of my ability. I will first give you two instances of what I conceive to be intended by the expression *'accidental'* when applied to killing.

"One case is that of a person carrying a loaded gun about. The gun goes off and shoots a bystander.—This is *'accidental killing'* and the person merely carrying about the gun ought not to be held responsible for the injury done by its going off. The other instance is that of a tree, which, when being cut down, falls unexpectedly to the cutter, and kills a bystander. This again is clearly *'accidental'* for which the cutter of the tree does not deserve to suffer.

"I will next acquaint you with my views of what is meant by *'killing in self-defense.'*

"A declares that unless B does a certain thing which A requires, that he will take B's life; or, B having already done an act offensive to A, A declares that he will kill B the first time he sees him. If B after such a threat, sees A approaching him with a gun, a knife, a stick,—in short, with any weapon or in any manner sufficient for the execution of his threat,—then the killing of A by B ought to be considered as killing in self-defense. Again—If B has a quarrel with A about a contract, or any subject whatever, and B sees A rushing towards him with a threat that he will take B's life, B in such a case ought not to be punished for killing A. The threat of A was accompanied with an action which made it appear that he would certainly execute it. B's killing of A would therefore be only in 'self-defense.'

" 'Wilful murder' is killing under any circumstances excepting such as were entirely independent of the slayer's consent, or, where threats have been received, or a rush made with a dangerous weapon in a threatening manner. There are degrees in 'wilful murder', which may mitigate its enormity. A person may be aggravated, and when maddened by passion, may destroy another;—or he may be in the habit of carrying pistols, a bowie-knife, and other weapons of offense about him, and may use them on slight provocations, merely because he has them about him. But, still, a death inflicted under such circumstances is a murder;—neither passion, nor the temptation from having arms about one, forms any excuse; no, not even drunkenness. No one has a right to put himself deliberately in either situation and hence he is liable to suffer for it.

"These are my views of the difference between the various sorts of killing. I will now relate what I think about evidence. Perhaps I can make myself best understood by giving you one story of an affair which happened in our own nation; and another of what once happened among the whites, both of which illustrate the meaning and effect of '*circumstantial evidence.*'

"What happened among ourselves took place at Amohy District, in our old nation.

"Two Cherokees had left their homes and had crossed a river to a distillery on the side occupied by the white people. We will designate one of them as M, and the other as R. Both drank at the distillery. R being intoxicated when he got to his cabin, fell out with his family. They withdrew from him and left him by himself; but they remained within hearing of him while they were lying out in the neighborhood; and they heard him making a noise till far into the night, when the noise ceased. On the next morning, the family went back to their house. R. was not there; or, rather, they did not see him there. But, alarmed, they sought around on every side, and found that the house was stained with blood. Upon the floor there was a pestle.[33] It was

---

[33]The heavy wooden implement with which the Indians crushed their corn in a wooden mortar.

bloody and upon its handle was the print of a hand in blood. They examined further. At length they found R. under the planks of the floor, dead. He was naked and covered with bruises, made, as they supposed, with the pestle. In their conjectures as to how this sad event could have happened, they presently thought of M., the man who had been left with R. at the distillery. They ascertained that M. had left there some time after night. At the river, they found on the Cherokee side a canoe belonging to the white. side; hence it was evident that M. had probably crossed the river. From the river-bank they tracked him to the yard of R.'s cabin. The way they tracked M. was this. M. was bare-foot. He had been frost bitten. From one foot he had lost the little toe; from the other, the big one. They traced the same foot prints from R.'s cabin to about six miles off in another direction; which search they completed early the next morning, where the foot-prints stopped, they found M. He had the dead man's hunting tunic on and his vest. They took him; and they saw that M.'s own clothes, as well as those of the dead man, were bloody; but they deferred any further examination at that time and made him remain with the clothing on, just as he was when they took him. He was brought before a court. His clothing was then searched. The family of R. proved that a part of it had been worn by R. the day before and up to the moment when they left him.

The same articles were also identified by R.'s neighbors. They were bloody.   As M. was being stripped before the jury, his own clothes also exhibited marks of blood, obviously made when he took up the dead body of R. to drag it under the floor.   Both the arms of M. were bloody and there was a line of blood across his arm and breast.   Upon this evidence M. was found guilty.   But no one had seen M. commit the crime and therefore the evidence was only *'circumstantial.'*   Five days afterward, however, M. confessed that he had committed the murder, precisely in the manner inferred, and he was hanged.

"The other occurrence, which was told me as having happened among the whites, is as follows:

"F. and G. were two strangers.   They met in travelling.   They shared one bed.   In the morning neither were to be found.   But from the bedside to a river some way from this house, there was a continuous line of blood, as if it had flowed from a severe wound; and at the river bank, the blood was seen more abundant than elsewhere; and then all further marks disappeared. The neighborhood was greatly excited.   Every attempt was made to discover one or both the strangers, but in vain.   At length G. was traced.   He could give no account of F.   Suspicion fastened on him as the murderer of F.—G. was thought to have dragged F.'s body from the house and to have flung it into the river.   He was tried and executed; and the evidence upon which he was convicted, was, like the former, only, '*circumstantial.*' Sometime afterwards, F. reappeared. He stated that, in the night, his nose had bled violently; that he hastened to the river bank to allay the bleeding, which had continued all the way; that he laid down upon the bank and fell asleep, and did not wake till he thought it was full time to proceed upon his journey; so not to lose a moment, he went on without going back to the house.

"You will perceive by these two cases of '*circumstantial evidence*' that though, in the first instance it convicted the guilty,—in the second, it destroyed the innocent. No matter how strong the proofs may appear, it is never prudent to condemn upon evidence merely '*circumstantial.*' An act for which a life is to be forfeited, should be seen and seen by more than one. This last is called '*point-blank evidence*'; and such evidence alone is entitled to your reliance in a case like the one at present before you."

The Chief Justice now withdrew, leaving the Jury by themselves, where they remained all day. At night, the High Sheriff came into Court and informed the Chief Justice that the witnesses had been brought back and were ready, which was communicated to the jury; and on Friday, December 25th, 1840, being

THE EIGHTH DAY OF TRIAL
the Jury sent to the Chief Justice, requesting that the

Creek interpreter should be summoned. The Chief Justice gave orders to the High Sheriff, who proceeded to summon the interpreters from their abodes several miles off; and on Saturday, December 26th, 1840.

THE NINTH DAY OF TRIAL,

the Jury came into Court, and the witnesses and interpreters being present, were re-sworn and re-examined. From the omission to note down by whom the respective questions were asked, I am at the same loss here, as on the former recapitulation of evidence; but the most important ones, I believe, as before, were put by the agents, or counsel, for the accused. The following is the report of the examination, as translated and taken down at the moment, in open court.

Soldier, a Cherokee, was the first produced; and after some skirmishing, as previously, between the parties, regarding his capacity, the interrogatories proceeded as follows:

Question. "Was you at the Creek camp when this affray took place?"

Answer. "I and some others were there."

Question. "Did you see them when they commenced the fight?"

Answer. "Yes."

Question. "How far were you from where they were fighting?"

Answer. "About eleven yards."

Question. "What did Archilla Smith have in his hand when they commenced fighting?"

Answer. "A knife."

Question. "What kind of a knife was it?"

Answer. "A large knife, about ten inches long."

Question. "What did MacIntosh have in his hand?"

Answer. "A switch."

Question. "Did Archilla Smith stab MacIntosh?"

Answer. "Yes."

Question. "Did you see him stab MacIntosh?"

Answer. "I saw him stab MacIntosh twice."

Question. "What did MacIntosh say when Archilla Smith stabbed him?"

Answer. "He called Peter and went a little further and called again."

Question. "How far from where they were fighting, to where MacIntosh fell from his horse?"

Answer. "About eighty-seven yards."

Question. "What is the name of the person that you say was with you?"

Answer. "Gay-Nu-Gay."

Question. "Where did you go when you left the Creek Camp?"

Answer. "I and Gay-Nu-Gay got on one horse and went towards Peter's and Archilla Smith told us to go with him to Peter's and he, Archilla Smith, would get whiskey. I and Gay-Nu-Gay did not wish to go to the house, but Archilla Smith urged us to go with him to the house, which we did; and on Archilla Smith's asking about Peter, he was told that he was not at home. Then we went toward Eagle's until we came to the forks of the road; then Archilla Smith went toward Eagles. I and Gay-Nu-Gay went towards Gay-Nu-Gay's mother's.

Question. "Where did you first see Gay-Nu-Gay?"

Answer. "Once in the old nation, when I was on my way to the Agency, I met him by somebody's field and Gay-Nu-Gay told me that he lived with George Hick's mother;—and the next time I saw him was at the Ohio river."

John, a Creek, was now re-produced for examination; and the Interpreters being placed by his side, he was sworn and interrogated as follows:

Question. "Was you at the Creek camp when Archilla Smith and MacIntosh had their affray?"

Answer. "I saw the affray."

Question. "How far from you did they commence their affray?"

Answer. "About ten yards. Archilla Smith overtook MacIntosh and took hold of the bridle and stabbed MacIntosh."

Question. "How often did he stab MacIntosh?"

Answer. "He stabbed him once. I do not know that he stabbed him more than once."

Question. "How long was the knife? And how broad was the blade?"

Answer. "About ten inches long and a broad blade."

Question. "Did you see him raise the knife and stab MacIntosh?"

Answer. "Yes. I saw him raise the knife and stab him."

Question. "Where did MacIntosh go after he was stabbed? Did MacIntosh say any thing after he went off?"

Answer. "I do not recollect that he said anything."

Question. "How far from where they were fighting, to where MacIntosh fell off?"

Answer. "About eighty-seven yards."

Question. "How long after MacIntosh was stabbed, before you saw him dead?"

Answer. "A short time after. Two men came by where he was lying and I went back with them to where he was lying and I saw him."

Question. "Was it dark when you went to see him?"

Answer. "Just after dark."

Question. "Did you examine him?"

Answer. "Yes."

Question. "Did you have a light."

Answer. "No."

Question. "Was the moon giving light?"

Answer. "No."

Question. "Did they take the body away that night?"

Answer. "Yes. Not long afterwards they took the body to Peters."

Question. "Were there any other people about there, drinking, at that time?"

Answer. "No. Only Soldier and Gay-Nu-Gay."

Question. "Who were the two men that found MacIntosh?"

Answer. "The Creek man Turtle; and the other was a Cherokee man; I do not know his name."

Question. "Who were they that took up his body?"

Answer. "I do not know. I did not see him until next morning, when I went up to Peter's."

Question. "What did those men do, that you went with to see the body of MacIntosh?"

Answer. "The Creek man stayed at my house that night, but I do not know what became of the Cherokee man."

Question. "Do you know whether MacIntosh and any other man had any difficulty that day?"

Answer. "No."

Sub-Be-Go, another Creek, was now brought forward again and, being duly sworn, was interrogated thus:

Question. "Was it at your house that the one killed the other?"

Answer. "Yes."

Question. "Who committed the murder?"

Answer. "Archilla Smith."

Question. "What did he kill him with?"

Answer. "A knife."

Question. "Was it light or dark at that time?"

Answer. "Just getting dark."

Question. "Did you see him stab MacIntosh?"

Answer. "Yes. It was done in the yard."

Question. "How many times did he stab him?"

Answer. "Once."

Question. "After Archilla Smith stabbed MacIntosh what did he do?"

Answer. "He immediately went off."

Question. "How far from the place where MacIntosh was stabbed, did he fall off?"

Answer. "About ninety yards."

Question. "How long after he was stabbed, or went off, before you saw him?"

Answer. "Not until next morning."

Question. "How long was the knife?"

Answer. "I did not see the length or size of the knife; but I saw the guard of the knife."

Question. "Did MacIntosh go off fast or slow, after he was stabbed?"

Answer. "He went off slow."

Question. "Did MacIntosh say any thing as he went off?"

Answer. "He did not say anything until he got close to the house."

Question. "Did you understand what he said?"

Answer. "Yes, He called Peter."

Question. "Did you see any blood the next morning?"

Answer. "He did not bleed right off; not until he got some distance. I saw the blood about forty steps from where he was stabbed."

Question. "Did you see the blood from that on to where he fell?"

Answer. "Yes."

Question. "Were you drinking whiskey at this time?"

Answer. "No."

Question. "Was that other witness drinking?"

Answer. "No."

Question. "Was Gay-Nu-Gay drinking?"

Answer. "He was not very drunk, but he was drinking."

The Jury again withdrew and at night came back into court.

The Chief Justice asked them if they had determined on their verdict.

The Foreman answered that they had.

Their names being then called over, they all stood up, and the Chief Justice asked them:

"Is Archilla Smith guilty or not guilty, of the murder of John MacIntosh?"

Answer. "Guilty."

VI

THE NINTH DAY: THE FATE OF ARCHILLA SMITH

The jury then took their places and the Chief Justice thus addressed the prisoner:

"Archilla Smith, after a most careful investigation, you have been found guilty by a jury of your country of having murdered John MacIntosh. You know the penalty of your crime; and, upon its enormity, it is unnecessary for me to dwell. But the last awful duty of my office now remains to be fulfilled; and would to Heaven you had been proven innocent instead of guilty, that I might have been spared the sad necessity of pronouncing upon a fellow-citizen, who has flung away such opportunities of being useful to his country, the last and dreadful sentence of the law: which is, that you, Archilla Smith, be retained in close custody until the expiration of five days hence, when you must be taken, on the first day of January, 1841, to the place which may be assigned for your execution, and, at the hour of twelve at noon, then and there be hanged by the neck until your body is dead, and may the Lord have mercy on your soul!"

The condemned, then, with perfect composure, and in a clear, firm tone, observed in Cherokee:

"You are every one of you old acquaintances of mine, Jurors. You have been several days engaged about my difficulty. But I have no hard thoughts against any one of you, Jurors, nor Judge, against you. I believe your object has been that my trial should be a fair one. I have, therefore, only one thing to say; and that is to the Judge. If the laws of the nation provide any course whereby I or my friends can petition the Principal Chief for my safety, so as to enable me to live again in peace, I would call upon the Judge to grant me that privilege. At the same time, I am aware that we are all alike subordinate beings. God is our Creator and he is my Master. If he has so ordered that I am to live on earth no longer, I am satisfied; and shall feel no disposition to complain of any one; for I was present, Jurors, when you were called upon to swear before your Creator that you would do justice in my case, and I believe you have decided according to what you think justice."

To this the Chief Justice replied in the ensuing terms:

"I will examine the law, If I find any such provision in it as you speak of, or if I can further any request or representation you may desire to make, you may rely upon my doing all I can for you, consistently with my sense of what is right and proper. In regard to petitioning the Principal Chief, I will let you know by twelve o'clock tomorrow what can be done."

The Court now broke up and the guard rode away with the condemned.

On the same evening, Saturday, December 26, 1840, when sentence was pronounced upon Archilla Smith the Chief Justice, consulted with the Foreman and some others of the Jury upon the subject of a petition to the Principal Chief for pardon, and they concluded that the evidence was of such a nature to forbid their sanctioning one. A letter to that effect was consequently drawn up in Cherokee and sent to the condemned. Meanwhile, both his advocates and some of his other friends moved actively in his favor.

During the progress of these efforts, Young Wolf, who had been Foreman of the Jury, and who is a native preacher of the Methodist persuasion, waited upon the condemned with the Reverend Mr. Worcester,[34] one of

---

[34]Rev. Samuel A. Worcester was born at Worcester, Massachusetts, January 19, 1798; he was graduated from University of Vermont 1819, and Andover Theological Seminary in 1823. He departed from Boston and arrived at Brainerd in the Cherokee Nation on October 21, 1825. After two years service here he went to New Echota, where he served as a missionary until September 16, 1831, when he was sentenced to the penitentiary by the Georgia authorities for his refusal to cease teaching the Cherokees or to subscribe to an oath of allegiance to the state and apply for a license to remain among the Indians. His conviction was reversed by the United States Supreme Court, and he was released January 14, 1833. He later transferred his activities to the Cherokee in the west where he arrived May 29, 1835. After a short stay at Dwight Mission he located at Park Hill December 2, 1836, and here conducted the work of the mission press and his church and mission activities. His press was the first in Oklahoma. He died at Park Hill April 20, 1859, and is buried in the little cemetery there. He was the grandfather of the late Miss Alice Robertson.

the missionaries.   They saw Archilla Smith two or three times.

At the first interview, Young Wolf felt some hesitation about approaching the prisoner.   Having been Foreman of the Jury by whom the prisoner was condemned, the preacher thought his presence might be objectionable and offered, if so, to withdraw.   Archilla Smith assured him that his concern was entirely ungrounded.   He had no prejudice whatever against Young Wolf as Foreman of the Jury.   He was convinced that the Foreman and the Jury had only done their duty and acted according to their views of justice. He thanked Young Wolf for having called with Mr. Worcester, and especially as he, being a Cherokee, could interpret between them, whenever they might be at a loss.

Some remark being made which Archilla Smith understood as tending to elicit from him an admission that he was guilty, he promptly exclaimed that he would never confess the act for which he had been condemned. He intimated that he was persuaded there would be hope from the interposition of the Principal Chief; and he asked if it was not the opinion of his visitors; to which they replied discouragingly, and begged him to make up his mind to the worst.   Mr. Worcester went, either on this occasion, or one of the later ones, into some conversation upon the affection and power of our Savior.

He asked the condemned, "What friend, among all those who so lately gathered round you, would, in your present situation, give up his life to save you? This has been already done for you by Jesus Christ; and it is within your own choice even now to avail yourself of that sacrifice." Archilla Smith listened with an air of intense interest and a sort of surprise. He thanked his reverend visitors most cordially for their attention and seemed much touched by it; but it did not appear to Mr. Worcester that even to the last he gave signs to be confided in of truly evangelical repentance.

A petition for pardon had, in the mean time, been drawn up by the friends of the condemned, and numerous signatures obtained to it, among which may be seen four of his last jury, which are printed in italics. The petition was as follows:

"To His Excellency, John Ross, Principal Chief.

"We, the undersigned citizens of the Cherokee Nation, having understood that Archilla Smith a citizen of this nation is condemned to be hanged on the 1st of January next, under a charge of murder,—therefore,—with a desire that peace and harmony may prevail, and with a due respect to the laws of the nation, would most humbly petition you, as the Supreme Executive of the nation, to interpose your power in the pardoning of said Archilla Smith.

Little Chicken
STAND WATIE
KA-HE-NA-KEE
THE STAFF
GEORGE H. STARR
T. J. PACK
J. A. BELL
DAVID BELL
THE SPEAKER
TE-HA-SA-TA-KE
JOHN CANDY
GEORGE W. ADAIR
CHARLES REASE
JAMES STARR
JOHN L. BALDRIDGE
JOHN SMITH
TAH-LAH-SU-NA
ELI CHU-GA-JUNT-
  NA
LUNEY BEAVER
ISAAC
OO-YAH-TAH
BEAR RUNNING
KA-TU-KES-KEY
GEORGE WATERS
JOSEPH STARR
KEEN-TO-KEE
TECUMPSEY B. STARR
CHU-SQUAH-LUN-
  TER
THOMAS STARR
BIG ACORN
FIELDS STARR
ELLIS STARR
CORN SILK
WILLIAM LASSLEY
SQUA-LO-LA
RUNABOUT

DROWNING BEAR
Samuel Chambers
JAMES CHAMBERS
George Chambers
JAY HICKS
JOHN SANDERS
DAVID SANDERS
ALEXANDER SANDERS
JOHN COLWELL
MOSES SANDERS
CHARLES SANDERS
ROBERT SANDERS
JOHN SEABOLT
BENJAMIN SANDERS
EDWARD SANDERS
Pigeon
ROBERT McLEMORE
ISAAC SANDERS
THOMAS B. WATIE
THOMAS SHADE
AH-KI-LO-NI-GAH
DAVID WATIE
JOHN A. WATIE
MANKILLER
AH-DOWEY
SAMUEL, MAYES
KIL-CHENE,
  his X mark
JOHN GRIFFIN,
  his X mark
SCOT MANKILLER
JOHN COX
WILLIAM TURNER
JOHN DOUGHERTY
GEORGE BLAIR
C. S. BEAN
EDLEY SPRINGSTON

CHARLES CRITTEN-
  DON
MOSES DOWNING
SAMUEL DOWNING
TA-QUOH
DAVID DOWNING
KUL-QUA-TA-KAY
CHE-SQUAH
LEWIS NELONIS
CHOO-NO-YAKEY
TOO-NOW-EY
JESSE MAYFIELD
J. A. RIDER
COOLEY SILK,
  his X mark
ARLEY LASLEY,
  her X mark
LEWIS GRIFFIN
NANCY FIELDS.
  her X mark
LUCINDY GRIFFIN
NANCY WHIRLWIND
LIDY GRIFFIN
CHINIPY
  his X mark
TE-SES-KY SILK
JESSEY OWENS
FOG SILK
MOLE
SEASON SILK
BENJAMIN
SIMON
WAR-PAR-CY SILK
COO-WAH-YAH
NEELEY McDANIEL
W. L. HOLT, J. M.
  SMITH."

With this petition, Stand Watie, William Holt,

(the counsel for the condemned), and George Washington Adair called at the house of the Principal Chief. On their presenting themselves, George Washington Adair desired a private conference.—It was granted. He produced the petition. The Principal Chief replied, that nothing would gratify him more than to feel that he was authorized to stay the execution; but the law was very explicit upon the subject, and it required the signatures of the Judge and Jury to entitle a petition to be received—which signatures were wanting—nor did the document even set forth one single reason why the criminal should not suffer. Under these circumstances, the Principal Chief had no power to act. George Washington Adair, in replying, pointed out some of the jurors' names among the signers of the petition, but continued that he was conscious of the objections which were likely to arise; that he had no power to remove them and only lamented that his interference must be fruitless. The rest of the party were very respectful to the Principal Chief; but it is said that William Holt, after he left the house, observed, "They must make two coffins instead of one; for if Archilla Smith is hanged, I will not survive him."

After hearing that the petition was rejected, the prisoner sent for Lewis Ross, the brother of the Principal Chief. He desired the good offices of Lewis Ross, who answered that it was not a case in which he

could interfere. Archilla Smith afterwards expressed
to his guards a wish to see the Principal Chief for the
purpose of getting his aid in drawing out a will.

John Ross was surprised just before dinner one
day, to see the whole cavalcade, with Archilla Smith
at their head, riding up to his gate.

Archilla Smith observed to the Principal Chief,
on entering the house, "I have desired to see you, sup-
posing you might interfere for my pardon."

"I have no discretionary power whatever" replied
John Ross,^{55} "to pardon a criminal. Here is .the law

^{55}John Ross was born at Rossville, Georgia, October 3, 1790,
and died in Washington, D. C., August 1, 1866. He was the son of
an immigrant from Scotland, by a Cherokee wife who was herself
three-quarters white. His boyhood name of Tsan-esdi, "Little John,"
was exchanged when he reached man's estate for that of Guwisgui,
or Cooweescoowee, by which was known a large white bird of un-
common occurrence, perhaps the egret or the swan. He went to
school in Kingston, Tennessee. In 1809 he was sent on a mission
to the Cherokee in Arkansas by Col. Return J. Meigs, the Indian
agent, and thence forward until the close of his life he remained in
the public service of his nation. At the battle of Horseshoe, and
in other operations of the Cherokee contingent against the Creeks
in 1813-14, he was adjutant of the Cherokee regiment under General
Jackson. He was chosen a member of the national committee of
the Cherokee Council in 1817 and drafted the reply to the United
States commissioners who were sent to negotiate the exchange of
the Cherokee lands for others west of the Mississippi. In the con-
test against the removal his talents found play and recognition. As
president of the national committee from 1819 till 1826 he was in-
strumental in the introduction of school and mechanical training,
and he led in the development of the civilized autonomous government embodied in the republican constitution adopted in 1827. He
was associate chief with William Hicks in that year, and president

on the subject (producing the law) ; and this will convince you that unless the judge, jury and neighbors of the party convicted, concur in the petition, I am not permitted to interfere;—I have no more right to move in the matter than any other citizen."

"I see now" answered Archilla Smith, "that it is not in your power to do any thing, and I suppose I must make ready for my fate."

Said John Ross, "I most sincerely hope that you will not give way to vain expectations of escape, but prepare yourself as well as you can to account with your God and to obtain his mercy."

As dinner time was approaching, the party determined to remain and take their dinner at the house. Archilla Smith, after John Ross had left the room, observed, "I will not trouble him about the will now; he is too much engaged in other matters."

It is supposed that the mention of the will was only an excuse to get to the Principal Chief.

Archilla Smith now sat awhile and looked over

---

of the Cherokee constitutional convention. From 1828 to the removal to the Indian Territory in 1839 he was principal chief of the Cherokee Nation, and headed the various national delegations that visited Washington to defend the rights of the Cherokee people to their national territory. After the arrival in Indian Territory, he was chosen chief of the united Cherokee Nation and held that office until his death, although during the dissensions caused by the Civil War, the Federal authorities temporarily deposed him (*Handbook of the American Indians*, II, 396).

some pages of the New Testament in Cherokee, which he took out of his pocket.

It was remarked, that, firm as his bearing was, his appearance had undergone the most extraordinary change for the worse within the last few days. But when dinner came on the table, he joined the Principal Chief, his family and the guard, and no one ate more heartily or unconcernedly than Archilla Smith. After dinner, he shook hands all round and departed with his escort.

On the night preceding his execution, he had David Carter,[38] the clerk of the court, with him, to draw up

---

[38]David Carter was born in North Carolina in 1802 of a white father and a Cherokee mother His father had been carried off by the Indians while a child and grew up with them. David came to the western Cherokee Nation in 1838 and became prominent in the affairs of his tribe; he served as associate justice of the supreme court, and later as chief justice, as superintendent of schools, and editor of the *Cherokee Advocate*. He died February 1, 1867 and is buried near the site of his comfortable home located on the old road running from Park Hill to Tahlequah. The venerable Mrs. Martha Tyner Swift of Muskogee told the editor that she can remember before the Civil War sitting on the fence in front of the home of her uncle David Carter and seeing John Ross drive by on his way to attend the National Council or other public duties in Tahlequah. Chief Ross, she said, was driven by a Negro driver and was attended also by a black boy as footman up behind, both in livery. They made a striking picture in the handsome carriage drawn by spirited horses in shining harness that the child never forgot. Carter often waited for Chief Ross to come along and then on horseback, beside the carriage, accompanied him into Tahlequah, exchanging the news of the day as they rode along. Carter's son, Benjamin W., removed to the Chickasaw Nation after the Civil War and there married Serena Josephene Guy, a sister of

his will. Archilla Smith was chained against the
side of the log prison. He was very minute in his instructions; enumerating debts he owed and debts which
were due to him. All his property was to go to his
three young sons,—his wife and elder children being
already well provided for; and none of the bequest to
the sons must be shared by any other members of the
family without the express consent of the legatees after
having reached an age capacitating them for the man-
agement of their own affairs.

It was near midnight when the will was about being
completed. The door of the log-prison was partly open.
Some of the guards stood around the fire, with their
backs to the condemned; others were here and there,
dozing. There was a bed by the side of the door. The
condemned remarked that he was weary and would be
glad to be loosened that he might repose on the bed.
His chain was unlocked. Nearly at the instance of his
approaching the bedside, the light dropped in the socket
and left all that side of the hut in shade. The footsteps
of the condemned appeared to quicken as the light ex-
pired and as he went near the bedside and the door.
One guard noticed the movement and glided between
him and the threshold. He paused, dropped back upon
the bed, and was silent.

Governor Guy of that nation, by whom on August 6, 1868, he
became the father of Charles D. Carter who represented his district in the United States House of Representatives.

It is supposed that he had been some time preparing for the opportunity; and, even as it was, had he moved an instant earlier, he might have sprang away, and in the dark, could, possibly, have escaped.

On the same evening, Stand Watie had attempted to bribe the very guard who thus stepped between Archilla Smith and the door. The man's name was Brown. "Brown," said Stand Watie, "five hundred dollars cannot be made every day." "No." "Would you not like to make five hundred dollars?" "Yes, as well as any one." "Contrive to leave Archilla Smith unwatched for a moment and it is yours." "I have too much respect for my own safety and my character, to sell either for five hundred dollars." "You have a brother. Perhaps you would not object to his having it?" "It is enough for me to answer for myself," said Brown, and turned away.

The morning of the first of January, 1841, had at length arrived. The log-hut where Archilla Smith and his guard passed the night, was about three quarters of a mile distant from the place assigned for the execution.[37] When the hour approached—"Here"—said Archilla Smith to a visitor—"take this pipe—I suppose I shall never want it again"—and presented the pipe which he had till then been smoking. He asked for a

---

[37]The Cherokee hanging tree was within the present limits of Tahlequah not far from the site of the Tahlequah light and power station.

drink as he was leaving the place, and observed, obscurely, as he went out, "I do not suffer for nothing."

A wagon had been prepared and a coffin placed in it. Over part of the wagon sides crossed a plank, and on the flooring, at its end, was a chair. The condemned sat in the chair.

When the party reached the place of execution, the gallows which had been ordered, had not come. The Sheriff saw that there would be no time to send for it; as it only wanted an hour and a half of twelve. He immediately fixed upon a tree as a substitute for the gallows. A large crowd had assembled; and among them were Archilla Smith's wife, daughter, aunt, sons, and, indeed, all his friends and relations male and female,—but not either of his two agents, Stand Watie, and William Holt. A grave was prepared; but the connections had been told that the family might have the body, if desired, some of them thought its removal useless; but an old aunt insisted on its being taken to their home.

Soon after the arrival of the cavalcade at the place of execution, a Cherokee dwelling near there was applied to for the loan of razors,—as Archilla Smith wished to shave himself before his death. The Indian replied that the Sheriff ought to be wary; as the condemned might mean either to take his own life or some other person's;—still, he would lend a razor on condition that proper precautions were adopted. It was thought as well, however, not to run any risks, and the razor was not handed to the condemned.

Twelve o'clock now approached. The cart was driven under the tree; and the Reverend Mr. Worcester, the missionary, and the Reverend Young Wolf, the native Cherokee preacher, appeared near it. The condemned seemed much gratified by their attention. He told them he could not die in peace without their prayers. As the fatal moment drew nigh, the Reverend Mr. Worcester, on being requested, offered up a supplication, which a person reported to me from memory. It was, to the best of his recollection, as follows:

"Almighty God! We see before us an awful instance of thy power. May it eventuate in an equally impressive exemplification of thy love. May the bitter fruit of the one sin for which atonement is now about to be exacted, procure the pardon of many. May it not only produce sincere penitence and consequent acceptance with thee, in the unhappy sufferer who now stands upon the threshold of eternity, but operate as a warning to all who either witness or hear of his fate. May it show this people to what dreadful results intemperance may lead; and when they see that the great commandment 'whoso sheddeth man's blood, by man shall his blood be shed' cannot be evaded; may it bring them to a salutary meditation through which all may be converted. In the name and through the mediation of our blessed Savior, we ask that the influences of the Holy Spirit may draw this blessing on the nation; and may the victim now offered up to the violated laws have cause to bless a doom, which if it awaken him to a proper knowledge of Thee and of himself will yet prove to him a happiness and a mercy into thy hands, oh blessed Savior, we commend his spirit."

Having ended, the Reverend Young Wolf, the native preacher, and who had been foreman of the last jury, arose, and uttered a prayer in Cherokee. The following is a translation of it, carefully made from the Cherokee, as afterwards repeated to me by Young Wolf himself.

"God of Heaven! Creator of all things! Thou, who knowest our inmost thoughts! I pray to thee have mercy on this man. He is standing on the threshold of death. He will presently leave this world to enter the world of spirits. Thou canst see into his heart. Thou art aware whether the charge for which he suffers is true or not. If he is guilty, I supplicate thee to forgive all his sins. Into thy hand we submit ourselves. We assemble together as a people to witness the death which our friend is about to suffer; and may it make us remember that we too, are born to die sooner or later, and prepare to meet thee in peace. May the view of thy power which we are now beholding, humble us before thee. May we continue humble. We are now about to part with our friend Archilla. We give him up to thee. May he receive thy pardon for his sins, that hereafter we may all come together again before thy throne and unite there in thy praise!"

The condemned now stood up in the wagon and addressed the bystanders in a clear and firm tone. He spoke in Cherokee; and there are ambiguities in his address, which I will mention after I have given the translation.

"Friends, I will speak a few words. We are to part. You will presently behold how evil comes. I do not suffer under the decree of my Creator but by the law passed at Tahlequah.—Friends, you must take warning.—I think, perhaps, that my being hated has brought me to this. No man can hope every time to escape; and the third I have been overtaken by the law. But avoid such practices.—I suppose I was preordained to be executed in this manner. I am ready to die. I do not fear to die. I have a hope, there, to live in peace. (*Tears now gushed from his eyes.*) I should not have shed tears had not the women come here to see me.—I have no more to say."

The Cherokees are divided in their construction of several parts of this address. Some of them understand the clause "no man can hope every time to escape; and the third, I have been overtaken by the law," to allude

to the three charges and chances of the trial;—the with-
drawal of the first jury, which gave him one hope of
getting clear;—the refusal of the second to proceed
without a fresh examination *viva voce* of witnesses,
which gave him another;—and his condemnation at the
third and final scrutiny.—Others, and the greater number, construe the clause as a dark admission that he
had twice deserved death for some undetected murder;
and that, for the third murder, was now "overtaken by
the law."

As soon as the address was ended, the people went
up, one by one, to shake hands with the condemned.
Presently, the High Sheriff observed that the hour of
execution being so near, he must beg that no more
would approach.

Precisely at twelve o'clock, the condemned was desired to step up on the chair and thence upon the plank
which crossed the wagon top. He did so and the rope
and the cap being adjusted, the wagon was driven from
under the tree. By some mal-adjustment of the rope,
it lengthened in such a manner, that the body trailed
upon the ground for an instant; but some Indians caught
the rope's other end, and instantly drew the body up.
The neck of the condemned was broken in the jerk and
he died forthwith and without a struggle.

The wife and daughter and female relations bore
the scene with considerable fortitude. But the three

young sons lost all command of themselves. They were loud in their lamentations.

The body remained hanging for an hour. It was then cut down and delivered to the relations, who conveyed it to the abode of the deceased.

————

Before dismissing this affair, I will mention a curious event remotely associated with it. Thomas Terrille, one of the Jury on the first part of the trial, and afterwards one of the guards on the second,—was himself killed in a drunken fray with another Cherokee by the name of Dennis Wolf, within somewhere about a week of the execution of Archilla Smith. Dennis Wolf was tried for murder and acquitted on the plea of the killing being accidental. Thomas Terrille waited on horseback for Dennis Wolf's return from the Court, meaning to take vengence under the ancient oral law, without heed of the more modern written one;—a memorable illustration of the extreme difficulty of overcoming a sort of inherent devotedness to this deepest rooted of all Indian prejudices.

Permit me to say that I have endeavored in the preceding narrative to give you as minutely accurate and as characteristic a picture as possible; and, in so doing, I have had more difficulty than any one can imagine, who has never experienced the impediments to gathering any sort of information in such regions, and especially where it must be obtained through Indian languages. In the present case, I have had to procure translations throughout from both Cherokees and Creeks; and to glean particulars from numberless sources, in addition to what I observed myself.

JOHN HOWARD PAYNE.

INDEX

Cherokee Indians in the West,
viii; guest of John Ross, ix;
difficulty of making transcript
of proceedings in Cherokee
court, 103.
Pheasant: 51.
Pigeon: 52, 91.
Point blank evidence explained:
78.
Prayers for Archilla Smith at
execution: 99.
Price, Looney: judge of Cherokee court, 7, 8, 14; charge to
jury, 44; emotions of, 46; in-
capacitated for second trial, 49.
Pritchet, James: 52.
Prisons in Cherokee Nation: 3.
Prisoners in Cherokee Nation,
method of holding: 3, 4.
Procedure in Cherokee court: 49,
55, 71, 72.
Prosecuting attorney: 13, 14.
Punishment in Cherokee Nation:
3.

Ratcliff, Richard: 51.
Rease, Charles: 91.
Removal of Cherokee Indians: 1.
Rider, J. A.: 92.
Rider, Thomas: 10, 11.
Ridge family: 1.
Ridge, Major: murder of, 58 n.
Ridge, John: murder of, 58 n.
Ross, Chief John: 4; described
by John Howard Payne, v;
sketch of, 93 n.; sketch of
home, 47 n., 48 n.; host of
Payne in Tennessee, vii; host
of Payne at Park Hill, ix;
home confiscated in Georgia, vi
n.; considers petition for clem-

ency, 92; visited by delegation
with Smith, 93; states the
Cherokee law on pardons, 94.
Ross's Landing: 1.
Ross, Lewis: home at Park Hill,
description of, 48 n.; declines
to interfere with operation of
law, 93.
Runabout: 91.
Russel, Jessee: 51.

Saddlerswell Theatre: iii.
Sanders, Alexander: 91.
Sanders, Benjamin: 91.
Sanders, Charles: 91.
Sanders, David: 91.
Sanders, Edward: 91.
Sanders, Isaac: 91.
Sanders, James: 91.
Sanders, John: 91.
Sanders, Moses: 91.
Sanders, Robert: 91.
Scene in Cherokee court room:
19.
Scott, Walter: iv.
Seabolt, John: 91.
Second trial of Archilla Smith:
51; opposed, 53; procedure, 55.
Self defense explained by judge:
73.
Sentence of court: 86.
Sharp: 10, 11.
Shelley, Mary Walstoncraft: iv.
Silk, Cooley: 92.
Silk, Fog: 92.
Silk, Season: 92.
Silk, Te-ses-ky: 92.
Silk, War-par-cy: 92.
Simon: 92.
Smith, Archilla: described, 5, 8;